The Parent and S
to Getting Into Medical School

By

Holly Johns

and

Elinor Johns

For Seren Beechey, with love.

Contents

Why you should read this book

This guide to getting into medical school is a joint effort, between Holly and her mum, Elinor. It is aimed at informing parents and students what is required when applying for a degree in Medicine at a UK medical school. It takes the reader through the process from GCSEs to the interviews in year 13 and gives an honest take on Holly's experiences. Holly received four offers to study Medicine from Cardiff, Birmingham, Sheffield, and Hull/York. This guide will tell you how she did it, and how you can too.

You don't need to doggedly read from start to finish – just jump to the chapter(s) you think will help most. But students (and their parents) setting out on their mission to become a doctor should read Chapter 1 as early as possible; ideally before choosing GCSEs, but definitely before choosing their A-level subjects.

As you will find out, this book is written as a conversation between Elinor and Holly and follows the timeline from first thinking about a medical career, to finally getting those Med School offers.

Most of the factual parts of the book were written by Elinor. Holly's insights as a future medical student are formatted like this:

HOLLY: *And this is what I thought!*

Key messages appear in a grey box like this:

 You really should take notice of this!

Foreword

This book tells you what we needed to know as Holly's parents; we learnt what was required as we went along rather than through strategic planning. I didn't see myself as a 'helicopter parent' or a 'tiger mum' but in my desire to help I had to learn how to be involved without being invasive. I went through this process stumbling through the fog of expectation always feeling a few steps behind others travelling the same path. Once Holly's offers came in, it seemed worth sharing our experiences to provide others with the insight we gained.

By the end of this book, you will have a clearer picture of what is required of a medical school applicant and of what you might do to help guide your teenager through the process.

It wasn't a given that Holly would pursue a medical career, even though she was ten when she first declared that she wanted to be a doctor. She mentioned it to my dad, a retired GP in the twilight of his life. "Oh, I don't think so," he said, chuckling. She was head to toe in sequins at the time and had just given a convincing performance as gin-sodden Miss Hannigan in a school production of 'Annie'. At that point, it seemed more likely that she'd be an actress or an alcoholic than a doctor, and like my aged pa, her year 6 teachers assumed her strength lay in English not Maths and hadn't taught her much Science at all. But Holly's interest was always there. When my friends displayed their children's paintings of ballet dancers or roses sewn in cross-stitch club, I kept quiet about Holly's fascination with drawing skeletons and told no-one she'd ordered a suturing kit from Amazon which came with its own fake flesh.

Later, when her secondary school prizes were in English and Drama, I assumed she would want to pursue the Arts and I advised her not to take separate sciences at GCSE; it took me a while to realise Biology was her passion and that she still wanted to be a doctor.

When Holly was 8 and I dragged myself through my first 5k race, she made a banner, intending to laud my unique talents. It read "Go, Mum! If you can do it, anyone can!" Two years later, after I waddled over the finish line of a half marathon she said, "You know mum, in a way your victory was my victory too." I understood what she meant, as any parent will, because we feel that way too; not just vicariously rejoicing in our child's every victory but wincing at every bump along the way. I didn't want Holly's quest to be a medic to be painful for either of us, but when Holly started sixth form studying Chemistry, Biology and Fine Art, with her career goal firmly in place, I was overwhelmed by the demands she now faced.

I imagine that, like me, you have a teenager who wants to be a doctor. This field is so competitive, you realise the hoops they have to jump through require the skill of an Olympic athlete. As the parent, whether you like it or not, you're the designated coach with no track record in this event. Well, don't worry, Holly was right: if I can do it, anyone can.

Hiya, I'm Holly! I'm writing this the day before I travel down to Cardiff to start my first year of Medical school. That is either because I thought it would be more poetic to write the beginning of this guide last, in sync with the start of my Medical course... or because I'm still pretty bad at time management. Let's pretend this is how I planned it!

Over the summer, I've been reflecting on how I succeeded in getting four offers to study Medicine. I also started getting some questions from younger students about MMIs, UCAT, work experience, University choices, Personal Statements... This made me put myself back into the shoes of a fresh-faced year 12. How did I feel at the start of this beautiful journey? Terrified, nauseous, and let's face it, probably a little sweaty. Because, although I was given a tremendous amount of support and advice from my family and my school, there were still tons of things I would have liked to have known when beginning this challenging journey.

I'll tell you what I did and try to help as much as I can with your medical application by means of giving you advice based on my experience of the process. However, I want to make it clear that I don't consider myself an outstanding candidate. I am no Oxbridge student. I am a very average person in terms of intelligence and skills and have to work hard to do well; by writing this guide, I just want to try my best to give an insight into how you too can survive the medical application process. I want this to be a fun guide, filled to the brim with honest anecdotes that I will probably regret putting in shortly after this gets published. I'm also hoping that by being very truthful in terms of my mistakes, I will also reassure you that you don't have to be the perfect student to get onto a course in Medicine!

Okay, let's grab our verbal reasoning skills and dive right in!

Chapter 1

What to consider first

Minimum Requirements – GCSEs and A levels

You need to start thinking about the implications of GCSE choices early and consider the likely results. Medical School admissions guidelines will often state that GCSE results must include a minimum of grade 7 (or an A) in Maths, English and Science. Holly was not penalised for taking Combined Science. Not one medical school had a problem with that. However, arguably, studying separate sciences at GCSE may prepare the student more effectively for the BMAT (Biomedical Aptitude Test).

Sorry to dive so early into Med School admission tests – but they can be influenced by GCSE choices, and can constrain which universities you can go to. There are two types of aptitude test. One is called the BMAT and has a dedicated section on scientific knowledge and applications.

The other aptitude test is the UCAT (University Clinical Aptitude Test) and has a different format where this was not an issue. We discuss the BMAT and UCAT tests later in the book.

If Holly had sat the BMAT she felt she would have been at a disadvantage because she had not studied as much Physics as students who had taken the three sciences separately at GCSE. Students can sit one or both aptitude tests in the summer holidays between year 12 and 13, depending on how much choice they want to give themselves in terms of where to apply. Chapter 4 has more details.

Remember that Med Schools set GCSE requirements as bare minimums and many applicants will have very high GCSE grades.

Even so, all is not lost if GCSE scores aren't as high as you would like. My friend's nephew hadn't done particularly well at GCSE but made up for this by getting an awesome score (above 700 average) on his UCAT aptitude test and got into Exeter. He avoided applying to some universities which placed a greater emphasis on GCSEs. For example, Cardiff will be unlikely to interview you unless you have a set of very high GCSEs. My mate Mel[1] told me about a really useful website where people exchange information about all sorts of university related issues called The Student Room which, up to this point, I had never heard of. The Student Room gurus showed compelling evidence to suggest that you needed a set of starred A grades or a set of 8/9s to get an offer when Holly applied.

---

[1] Everyone needs a friend who is willing to disseminate their knowledge, ideally someone who has just been through the process, or like Mel, someone who can retain a lot of information and is willing to share the anxious moments!

Luckily, Holly got grade 9 (or top starred A) in English Literature and Language, Art and Double Science and 8 (Low starred A) in Maths, Drama, History, Geography and RS but she hadn't taken a language. We discovered too late that this meant that she would be at a disadvantage if she were to apply to UCL. She could still have applied but would have had to commit to learning a foreign language as part of her course if she'd been offered a place.

A-level choices are fairly straightforward, but there is flexibility regarding the third choice.

Most medical schools require only three A levels, including at least two science A levels, with the sciences being Chemistry and/or Biology. You need to check the specific requirements for each course on their admissions website.

UEA, for example, cites only Biology as compulsory. Some universities like Manchester, Keele, Oxford and Cambridge are keen that the third subject is a 'rigorous academic subject'. We were excited to discover that medical schools such as BARTS, Hull/York, Cardiff, Brighton and Leeds said they welcomed a broader third subject from the Arts/ Languages or Humanities. [2]

I had thought Holly would do English Literature as a third A level but Holly asked me to check whether Art was acceptable. I rang admissions at five medical schools stressing that it was Fine Art that my daughter

---

[2] On their published admissions information only Brighton, Hull/York, Plymouth and Aberdeen explicitly welcomed Arts or Humanities subjects as the 3rd A-level, but when I rang admissions at other universities, they also confirmed that they accepted Arts. If in doubt, phone them up!

was intending to study. "It's largely a practical course, though. Are you sure?" I repeated – my bias stemming from my own past as an English teacher. The exasperation on the other end of the phone was becoming palpable – I hung up quickly, realizing I needed to stop projecting my own passions on my daughter and accept the fact that Holly wasn't going to be studying any more Shakespeare. I had randomly selected five universities to ring and she had to make only four choices; that seemed good enough to both of us at the time and Holly was delighted.

Despite her love of Art, Holly felt a pang of loss at discarding English and History but there wasn't any value in doing a fourth A level. The offers were always going to be based on three A levels and her time was precious, so it seemed better to …

Simply focus on getting three A grades, including the compulsory Chemistry and/or Biology!

For the more mathematically minded, note that:

Further Maths was generally not acceptable as a separate qualification if you are already studying A-level Maths. Further Maths may be on your CV as fourth A level, but Med Schools will ignore it as part of their offer. Bear in mind that you can complete a medicine degree with good GCSE maths.

Also:

None of the universities would accept General Studies or Critical Thinking for the third A level.

Oxbridge

Holly hadn't ever considered applying to Oxford or Cambridge but I have added this info for those of you who might be interested.

Oxford's medical course is of six year duration including a 3 year BA. The A level requirement is A*AA with an A in both Chemistry and one more out of Biology, Physics, Maths or Further Maths. Typically, 26% of applicants are interviewed and only 9% are successful. The annual intake is around 154.

The interviews are described as conversations about your chosen subject – like a short tutorial with someone who knows a lot about it. They are designed to assess academic potential, to see how well you can approach a new problem, not how much you already know. Having said that they will expect your thinking to be based on sound scientific principles.

Cambridge also offers a six year course and will interview around 80% of applicants but obviously the competition at interview is very strong. Despite the much higher proportion of applicants being interviewed, the rejection rate at interview is also higher since only 16% of applicants emerge with an offer. Around 280 places are available each year. Like Oxford, the interviews are very different from the standard MMI [multiple mini interview] format of other universities. Cambridge focuses on academic excellence rather than medical training, ethics, or the demands of being a doctor. The interviews are given individually and involve hard science and maths questions with two tutors.

The aptitude test requirement for Oxbridge applicants is the BMAT. The BMAT can be taken at the end of August or in the October half term.

Beware! If candidates take the BMAT in October they will not know their result before sending off their UCAS application, so the August test is far preferable to avoid wasting a UCAS selection.

The BMAT and UCAT tests are discussed more in Chapter 4.

The Extended Project Qualification (EPQ)

Many schools will offer sixth form students the option of doing an Extended Project Qualification alongside their A levels. This is not to be confused with the Level 3 EPQ that can be taken alongside GCSEs which is not valued in the same way.

If you are lucky, your school will allocate some time-tabled lessons and a mentor to help advise and guide the student through their EPQ. The EPQ is completed before the Year 13 exams, but the precise timing will be dependent on the school. In Holly's case the final presentation had to be delivered at the end of September at the start of Year 13. During the Spring and Summer term of Year 12 Holly had to decide on her title, log her progress exploring her research and thought processes and complete the essay in the format of a research paper. She also had to create a Powerpoint presentation.

Students can do an EPQ on any topic they like but it made sense to make the EPQ connected to the field of medicine so that it was something to link to work experience and areas of interest that she could draw upon in her personal statement and in the interviews.

Holly chose to focus on advancements in prosthetics, having seen amputees on the renal ward at the Lister Hospital, Stevenage, where she volunteered. She gained her official starred A for her EPQ in January 2020.

This certificate was the equivalent to half an A level; it was useful because both Sheffield and Hull/York admissions would 'trade' an A-grade EPQ for a single A-level grade drop as long as she had A grades in the other subjects. Holly was less confident in Chemistry than she was in Art and Biology, so it was reassuring that she could get in with AAB. However, Hull/York were offering this only if she put them first. Sheffield, on the other hand offered this without any caveats. This contributed to her decision to put Sheffield down as her insurance choice.

HOLLY:

Doing an EPQ was awesome, 5 stars on Trip Advisor for sure. Not only does it give you an excuse to procrastinate doing Chemistry homework by really delving into a medical topic you're passionate about, but it is also something you can bring up at interview. I used it at least once at every MMI circuit I did. They might ask you something like:

- **Tell me about a time where you self-directed your learning?**

  Nice, you can launch straight in with your EPQ journey - dazzle them with how you were able to develop effective time management skills with your Gantt chart and time management diary.

- **What attributes do you have that will make you a good Doctor/ medical student?**

  Always be sure to back up your 'attributes' with evidence - anything like 'inquisitive' or 'independent learner' can be backed up with your EPQ.

- **Why do you want to do this medical course?**

  One of the reasons you might give is that you have had a taste of the doing independent research from doing your EPQ and so that aspect of the course - particularly if the University is offering PBL (Problem Based Learning) or CBL (Case Based Learning) - really attracts you.

- ***What is one of your weaknesses?***

Argh, that's a gross question and I never actually got asked that but if I did, I would probably swing it like this:

*"I definitely acknowledge that I have a real weakness in public speaking; I always tremble, look at the floor and speak too fast. But I recognise this and have taken strides to correct this weakness. I am improving this by always volunteering first for presentations in class and **took part in the EPQ** despite knowing that this would mean I'd have to give an in-depth presentation to the class about my chosen subject. As a result, I am much more confident when speaking publicly but I would still like to improve further as I know I will need this skill to be a doctor, as I saw from my volunteering experience…"*

You get the gist.

Bottom line is that, yes, it's quite a hefty bit of work, but you'll be very grateful for it in the long run. If your school doesn't do it or you would rather focus your study time on your A Levels, it still might be worth doing some additional in-depth research on a topic that you're passionate about. Alternatively, enrol in a little online course alongside your A Levels. This way you can substitute that independent learning for the EPQ in the answers above.

Chapter 2

Finding relevant medical or care experience

Holly had joined St John Ambulance cadets in the Autumn term of year 11 but hadn't done anything else in terms of relevant work experience. After the GCSE exams were over, she spent a lot of time at the library helping children to complete the summer Reading Challenge. This was something which might have been worth drawing on to show she had good communication skills but she also needed something in a medical setting. At school she was given a leaflet about the things she needed to consider if applying for medicine.

My heart banged as I read that the leaflet advocated long term commitment in a variety of settings including a GP practice, a hospital, and a care home. My mate Mel, who knew enough about applying for medicine to make it her specialist subject on 'Mastermind,' explained that Holly should try and volunteer with a variety of groups: the young, the elderly, and the sick or needy. Holly's new form tutor also told me that medical schools were very interested in students who had shown a long term commitment to volunteering work.

All this made sense but threw me into a perpetual state of anxiety. How would Holly be able to get these volunteering posts? Where would she find the time? She had only 9 months before having to complete her university application (UCAS form) so how could she compete with students who had started volunteering much earlier? The boy I knew of, who had got into Exeter the previous year, had been volunteering at the same care home for three years. How could Holly compensate for having left it so late?

I spent months gnawing my knuckles, ruminating over my inability to help Holly to find a place to volunteer earlier. In the summer before starting year 12, I had, in fact, tried to organise something alongside the Reading Challenge at the library. I had contacted a suitable place, erroneously thinking it was a hospice where someone else's daughter had volunteered a few years previously. The application form arrived just hours before we were due to leave on our fortnight's holiday. I plunged headlong into making contact on Holly's behalf, my pulse racing as I realised how little time I had to organise referees, get a DBS[3] check done and find out where I'd stashed the family's passports. Sounding desperate and slightly deranged, I messed up the phone call.

Unsurprisingly, they fobbed me off saying they weren't interested in applying for Holly's DBS check, pointing out that I had misunderstood the nature of the support needed and suggesting there was no point in Holly applying if she was unable to help in the weekdays from September anyway. I came off the phone feeling like a fool. I hadn't even thought about the time it would take for her to get a DBS check done, nor had I considered that these busy institutions might find it

---

[3] A criminal background check. The Criminal Records Bureau (CRB) and the Independent Safeguarding Authority (ISA) have merged to become the Disclosure and Barring Service (DBS) so CRB checks are now called DBS checks. Vulnerable groups of people need to be protected and these DBS checks are crucial in ensuring the most suitable people are appointed to voluntary (or paid) roles working with these groups. Be aware that this can take a few weeks to come through. Once your teenager gets a DBS certificate for one placement, it is a good idea to immediately apply to get it extended to cover the whole year.

impossible to use volunteers usefully unless they could commit full days to helping. I realised that they also wanted someone mature enough not to need their mum to make enquiries for them. I learned my lesson and backed off.

It can take weeks to get a DBS certificate, so do it early. Apply for a Basic DBS Check – this will cost around £20 with a smaller annual update fee. This should be accepted at most placement organisations, unless they specify a company-specific DBS Check. There may be a reduced fee for volunteer (unpaid) work – see: www.gov.uk/government/publications/disclosure -application-process-for-volunteers/

At the time, Holly was a typical, self-conscious sixteen year old, but from this point on, she used her initiative to email, speak to people on the phone, and filled in her own forms. It was an important learning curve for her, especially in terms of phone etiquette. Up until then cryptic texts and 'likes' were her mode of communication; she had little experience of calling up friends, let alone strangers and she found it excruciating at first.

I was amazed how quietly she spoke on the phone and how abruptly she signed off. I got her to practise winding up a conversation in both formal and informal situations, getting her to express gratitude and enthusiasm in both words and intonation. She needed to learn to weave in conventional, gentle repetitive phrasing, "Thank you so much, I look forward to hearing from you... Good-bye... thank you for your time, goodbye..." Basically, I teased her mercilessly until she got the idea.

HOLLY:

Cruel but true!

I did need the telephone training, and it was better for me to take charge of finding placements. It would have been useful to have set something up for the holidays after my GCSEs.

*If I could go back in time, **I would have definitely made a few enquiries as early as February half term of year 11** so that I could have used that long break to volunteer in a medical setting.*

On the plus side, I really enjoyed volunteering at the library that summer and I could have referred to this as a valid example of my displaying good communication skills and empathy with young children in my personal statement and interviews if I hadn't had other experiences to draw on.

Students should start searching for placements as early as February in Year 11, with a view to volunteering in the long holiday after GCSE exams.

Where to volunteer?

Truthfully, I relied on marvellous Mel. She got her information from social networking sites like The Student Room, and Mumsnet, and drew on her sociable persona which meant she knew what others in the area had done when their kids were applying for medicine. Luckily, she spent hours soaking up the knowledge and then, at regular intervals, I squeezed it back out of her.

HOLLY:

Yeah, my mum really needed to chill out over this. Exasperated sighs, mutterings of 'you don't have enough' and comparisons of my inferior medical portfolio to that of others probably wasn't my favourite soundtrack during this time.

*If you're struggling to find a load of placement experience related to Medicine, please don't despair! I was really fortunate in getting the amount of medically related volunteering and shadowing experience I ultimately got but I think that it's important to stress that **you do not need tons of it.** There is only so much you can put into that Personal Statement and can squeeze into the 5-8 minutes of interview time at each interview station. Also, the Universities will appreciate that medically related work experience can be very tricky to come by.*

In addition, as you've read above, one of the key points of anxiety for my mum and myself was the fixation on the amount of time I had been volunteering. Some people have been doing things like St John Ambulance cadets since they were 7 so we were a little nervous about this because I had joined only in year 11. But in all honesty, I think having 1-2 years of regular voluntary/work experience is fine; it shows you have that commitment box checked. At least two of my friends had less than a year of regular volunteering experience and still got offers from Med schools.

From my experience, I would argue that **they care more about what you learned and what you can reflect on from these experiences rather than how many weeks you spent volunteering.** *Certainly, at interview I usually didn't name drop the X number of weeks I spent at a certain place every time I mentioned my volunteering experience and I don't think they particularly wanted me to. So please don't panic!*

On the flip side, if you're a kid who's been an avid SJA cadet since you were an embryo and you still enjoy it, then that can only be a good thing and you can totally bring that up on your personal statement and in your interview.

Even if you can't arrange a medical or care related experience, almost any volunteering work or part-time job will be evidence of time management and interacting with other people. Don't just think abstractly about those experiences; when you get home write down the specific circumstances; what was the issue, what did you do and say, how did others react, how do you think they felt, and how did you feel afterwards? There may be times when all went well, but just as valuable is when it didn't and you learned something about yourself and other people. These anecdotes will help you in the interviews, so <u>write them down!</u>

Chapter 3

Getting the most out of volunteering

I knew Holly would need to cram her volunteering experience into the academic year, from September to July of year 12. In fact, she was able only to manage one week's worth in the summer between year 12 and year 13. We knew that during this period, she would need to sit her UCAT and/or BMAT aptitude test before applying to her chosen universities. Preparing for this incredibly difficult exam would take up a lot of the summer holidays.

In the October half term of year 12 Holly used her initiative and emailed a local day hospice for cancer patients. She spoke to the hospice on the phone and was then interviewed for a role as a volunteer. This was something she could do only in her holidays, at Christmas and in the Spring term as they wanted her only on Thursdays and Fridays and for full days. As a result, Holly spent only six days at the hospice in total, but they were long enough to make a significant impact on her. She was taken on a home visit and was expected to sit in on the Friday supervision meetings but spent most of her time chatting to patients and joining in their activities, developing her skills of communicating with chronically ill patients, and gaining some understanding of a multi-disciplinary team and its function.

Holly also benefitted from following in Mel's son's footsteps. The first crucial information came when Mel told me her son Toby was doing a three-month placement at the Lister hospital. I told Holly and suggested she should Google volunteering at the Lister and find out how to apply. This was relatively painless; it required some form filling and attendance at an induction day.

Just before she got the placement, I was chatting to an acquaintance, Michelle, a senior diabetic nurse. She kindly offered to take Holly to work, into her health clinic for a day. This turned out to be fortuitous as Holly was allocated the renal ward for her three-month stint at the Lister and was able to see links between mismanaged diabetes and dialysis treatment. Holly volunteered on the same ward between 9 and 12 every Saturday. Her main role was to help the housekeeper to hand out drinks and biscuits and to help with food orders. Significantly, she was also able to chat empathetically to patients and to observe doctors and nurses who visited the ward while she was there. It was here that she saw amputees who suffered phantom limb pain and discomfort from their prosthetics. Her concern for them led to her decision to base her EPQ project on developments in prosthetics.

Holly had joined St John Ambulance cadets in the autumn of year 11. Luckily, her St John Ambulance leader worked at the Lister and was kind enough to organise a week of shadowing in a variety of departments for all those cadets who were applying for medicine. It was during this week of shadowing in December of year 12 that Holly gained a lot of experiences that she could reflect on for her personal statement and for the interviews. Holly watched an emergency tracheostomy take place, had to leg it through the hospital following a nurse who was running to an emergency in the hospital car park, and got up close and personal with a kidney being removed in theatre. I had never seen her so fired up with enthusiasm for the profession, but in her innocence and naivety she also had a few experiences that in hindsight made her cringe; all of these mixed emotions turned out to be just as

21

useful to draw on, and to reflect upon in interviews. Crucially, during this week of shadowing she had her first taste of being asked by medical professionals why she wanted to do medicine and stuttered her way through unprepared answers wondering how she could express herself in a manner which could do this question justice. Every medical candidate needs to work out a concise but thoughtful response to this key question.

The three-month stint in the Renal ward had come to an end and Holly was intending to ask for an extension, perhaps on a different ward when Mel told us some exciting news. Her son Toby had been accepted on the Empathy Project. The project was running at Hertfordshire hospitals, including the Lister. So, in the spring term Holly applied, was interviewed and trained to be a 'peer supporter' based in A&E.

In small teams, she would wait to see if teenagers came into the waiting room. The team was meant to listen to the teenagers' concerns and signpost them to support services where appropriate. They would also support on the children's ward if there was no-one age appropriate to support in A&E. The students were closely monitored and had to complete detailed feedback sheets for their supervisors after their weekly three hour stint, reflecting on what had been difficult and what had gone well. Although there were evenings where Holly and her buddies hadn't been able to do much more than make people coffees, there were other occasions when they had come into contact with vulnerable adolescents and had been successfully supportive. This led to Holly being nominated by her Youth Connections supervisor for a Stevenage Borough Council Award. Although she didn't win it, it made her feel valued. It also meant that she had some concrete proof of her empathy in a relevant setting.

The final shadowing opportunity came as a result of my friend Dom inviting us round to meet her bestie, Nicky, a general metabolic specialist nurse at Great Ormond Street. This was an amazing, lucky contact to make. It was like telling a friend that you wanted to get into acting and finding out that their best mate was running the Oscars and would let you go back- stage to meet Brad Pitt.

By now, Holly was revising like crazy for her end of year exams, knowing she had to impress enough to get those three A grade predictions from her teachers and aware that she had an enormous amount of work to do to get through the aptitude tests at a competitive level. The only way she could fit in the week of work shadowing was by doing it in the last few days before going back to school. Thankfully, this was possible. Holly completed the relevant forms and acquired the references just in time and her DBS was still valid. The week at Great Ormond street was one of the experiences she drew upon most for her personal statement and her interviews because of the patients and staff she observed interacting; she was so grateful for that opportunity.

Find out what work shadowing or volunteering opportunities may exist in your area. Think about places where people need help - care homes, hospitals, day centres, after-school clubs, pharmacies, libraries, or shops. Ask friends, relatives, or your social media groups for healthcare contacts you could ask to shadow for a couple of days. Be prepared to be interviewed for part-time work or volunteering, as they will need to assess your suitability. You don't need to write a detailed diary – instead reflect on specific events when you observed or learned something interesting about yourself or professionals in a care setting.

HOLLY:

*What I didn't truly appreciate until I'd gotten to the stage of preparing for the MMIs is that what matters more than the abundance or the type of work experience you gained is what you **learned and reflected** on it. In other words, you can take the same anecdote and twist it in a way that you can apply it to many different MMI stations or interview questions.*

*For example, say you sat in at a clinic with a Paediatrician, let's call him Dr. Babykins, and he's talking about the next steps regarding the treatment of an ill baby with their parents. One of the questions at the first station asks about the different qualities needed in a doctor, (needless to say you should slip in some of your volunteering/shadowing experience here). Great! Tell them about his **amazing communication skills**, how he spoke clearly, how he had an open manner, retained eye contact, asked them questions to check their understanding, nodded and listened thoughtfully and reassured them etc.*

*A different station might ask why you want to do medicine. Again, you can bring up Dr. Babykins and how sitting in on his clinic inspired you and showed you how diverse the skills required were as, not only did he have to have impeccable communication skills (you can go over these again), he also had to be a **good teacher** at a **basic level** for the parents, explaining how the treatment would work, and answering their queries regarding the illness.*

*You noticed he was also **adaptable** in teaching the more **complex** side of the case to a junior doctor. Not to mention how you got a taste of just how broad, varied and **interesting** the academia behind the diseases can be by asking Dr. Babykins about the patient's illness afterwards. Developing these skills and learning about the biology behind these illnesses really draws you to Medicine. The prospect of being able to one day potentially emulate Dr. Babykins would be so fulfilling.*

What I'm trying to say is that you can reflect on just one experience in many different ways and potentially re-use these during the MMI circuit. Each station is manned by a different set of interviewers who knows nothing about you. They are not the same people who selected you for interview and will not have seen your application. Remember that at each station you are starting from scratch.

Another point worth mentioning is that ANY work experience, from volunteering in a charity shop to tutoring to having a part-time retail job, is something you can use at interview. You can use it to show that you have great time-management skills (you can balance your studies with the demands of a part-time job) or that you have excellent communication skills (as a peer supporter you taught another student photosynthesis by speaking clearly and slowly, asking them questions along the way to make sure they understood) and that you can work cohesively with a team. Interviewers will always be expecting you to back up any claims you make about yourself with evidence and these anecdotes are great for doing that.

The parent's role

My role in all this was mainly as taxi driver. I drove Holly to Stevenage and to the train station and it was often on our car journeys that I asked her about her experiences. The recounting was important because it allowed her to reflect on her role and that of others. Of her own volition, she assiduously made notes on her experiences and promptly lost them amidst the tsunami of books and A4 paper engulfing her bedroom. Even so, the mere process of making notes was helpful when it came to analysing what she had learned from her volunteering experiences.

HOLLY:

I was really indebted to my mum (and dad) for all the lifts as this was incredibly helpful!

I have a January birthday and eagerly took some driving lessons, hoping I could soon drive myself to my volunteering placements. As each lesson passed the more my instructor pleaded with me ("Please, Miss Holly! Slow down – you are giving me a heart attack!"). Fearing for the level of my instructor's blood pressure and the safety of pedestrians, I gave up lessons and relied on my mum to get me from A to B.

> *As a parent one of the best ways to support your med kid is to give up some of your time to help take them to their work experience placements and interrogating them about it afterwards. I appreciate this might not be possible if you don't have a car or if you have a busy work life, but if you can help arrange a lift share to and from the hospital for your kid then it's one less obstacle in their way in getting that invaluable experience. In addition, your med kid will probably have a lot on their plate, so car journeys back from the hospital can be a great time to talk about what you have just seen and reflect on what you've learned.*
>
> *I actually tried recording some of these talks on my phone so I could play them back when I needed it later on in the year. This leaves time for more studying when you get home! Oh, and more time for sleep...*

Obviously, it is helpful to have medical or healthcare contacts in the family if they can open doors to shadowing opportunities, but they need to be in an appropriate field to help directly. Even then, this isn't a guaranteed aid to success. I heard of some applicants who were unsuccessful in gaining interviews and were ultimately rejected despite having really good medical contacts.

We have two psychiatrists in the family – my brother and sister-in-law. My brother had already retired but his wife was still a highly successful, impressive CEO. Holly was lucky enough to spend a day with her in the Easter holidays of year 12, going from meeting to meeting and coming into contact with some very prestigious, high-powered people who asked her again why she wanted to study medicine and be a doctor - a question she still struggled to answer concisely and cogently!

Holly was extremely grateful to have the opportunity to shadow her aunt for the day and it added to her list of insights but in reality she wasn't able to draw as much from her high powered connection as she was from the placements that she had sorted out herself. On the other hand, she was lucky that she could ask her uncle and aunt what they considered to be the significant issues affecting the NHS. She also tried to read up on current issues in the media but undoubtedly, discussing her views with adults was important in gaining clarity of thought and enabling her to articulate her views as she would have to do in her interviews.

It is the teenager who should use their initiative to organise work shadowing or volunteering placements. Parents can help by pointing them in the right direction.

Holly:

I am hugely thankful and fortunate that I had people in my family who were medical professionals and were willing to give me some invaluable insight into the profession.

*However, I'm here to tell you that **not** having family connections can actually work in your favour! Interviewers want to hear that you were so **interested, independent and curious** about the healthcare service that you went out of your way to find out how you could volunteer for that hospice or how you called up your local hospital to ask if you could do any volunteering there.*

I ended up talking at the interview about the experiences where I had more of an active role and the experiences that I had independently organised, rather than what I did the day I followed my Aunt around like a scared chihuahua.

I'm not saying you shouldn't exploit your connections; you should always exploit any resources you have to get a better insight into medicine. Exploit your family for sure - it's what they're there for ;) . But in addition to this make sure you grow the confidence to ring up the hospitals, the youth organisations, the hospices and organise it yourself. I know this can be really daunting- my mum wasn't lying about my ineptitude on the phone earlier - but I promise, putting yourself in situations where you're uncomfortable is a staple part of the Medical Application Diet and the more you do, the better you'll get at it!

Chapter 4

The Aptitude Tests:
BMAT or UCAT?

My husband, Simon, had bought a couple of books on these tests for Holly while she was studying for her GCSEs but decided not to show her the content until after her results because the tasks were so difficult. (A comparison of the two test structures appears in the Appendix). From time to time Simon and I amused ourselves trying to work out the connections between shapes and patterns and failing spectacularly.

HOLLY:

The UCAT exam... (cue Hitchcock movie music).

At the start of Year 12, the medical application process seemed to be this tortuous labyrinth and I knew exactly who the Goblin King was - a much less fun, less sparkly David Bowie stood between me and my dream of becoming a Medical Student. The Goblin King in question is of course the UCAT.

The knowledge that I would have to sit this insanely difficult exam that was going to be unlike anything I'd ever been tested on before was probably the most terrifying thing about the medical application process, at the start. I was absolutely dreading it, particularly the quantitative reasoning section. My mental maths had deteriorated at such an exponential rate since sitting my GCSEs... you wouldn't even be able to log it. But with months of preparation and the right tools for the job even I was able to do sufficiently well in the UCAT; so never fear! You will be just fine.

I've given my thoughts on the different resources used for the UCAT in the Appendix and I've tried to list them in the order I used them. There is so much advice and so many resources out there for the UCAT, which is a huge help, so make sure you use them. If you're on a budget, there are some free resources available in the form of YouTube videos (Kharma Medic's YouTube videos were life-saving) and the Official UCAT website has some online resources which are definitely worth doing. But I would strongly suggest saving for 1-2 months' worth of Medify which is an online resource bursting with questions and mocks.

My main advice for the UCAT:

1) *DON'T PANIC. You might have run a diagnostic mock test right at the start of your UCAT preparation and perhaps you're in the 400s for some of the sections. You will improve massively with practice- in some areas I improved by around 200 points over 6 weeks. So don't worry, hug your pillow, eat a Twix and do some more questions!*

2) *Make time to practise. Hopefully, you've got a lot of time during the summer for some really hardcore UCAT practice. I left myself about 6 weeks to really get into the UCAT, I did a couple of hours a day and increased this amount as I got closer to my deadline. Try to do at least 2 hours every day as you'll want to get your mind, body and soul ready for the intense pressure of that 2 hour exam.*

3) *It's difficult to recommend how many weeks exactly you should do as you might be particularly adept at aspects of the UCAT and not need as much time as I did. I think that's why it's good to do a diagnostic mock fairly far away from your UCAT date- it will give you a rough idea of how hard you need to work to improve your score. Most websites recommend 4 weeks minimum for the average student but, ideally, I would say do 6-7 weeks. This is why online question banks and mocks are so invaluable- you will be able to practise keyboard shortcuts, staring at a bright screen for hours, muttering death threats at a virtual calculator... I beg you to practise for at least a solid 4 weeks with these online questions.*

4) *Personally, I'd decided I'd make my way through the books for the first week or two and then do a load of online question banks and online mocks using Kaplan, Medify and the Official UCAT website. I would recommend just paying for Medify rather than Kaplan as it was the closest online resource, second only to the UCAT's own official website, that comes to mimicking what the UCAT was actually like.*

5) *Identify your weaknesses. Medify will actually help you a lot with this as it does a breakdown of all your past sets of questions and analyses all your past performances in cute little graphs for each section. Once you've identified that you are worse than a toddler at the QR section (speaking from personal experience) you will focus more heavily on QR from then on. Then in each section make sure you determine which types of questions you are also particularly weak on- for example, in QR, anything to do with taxes or train timetables used to make me nauseous, so I had to practice those ones in particular.*

6) *Triage the questions. A crucial tip given by Kharma Medic.* **All the questions in UCAT are worth the same number of marks!** *Flag the harder questions, move on and return to them only if you have the time - harvest those easy marks first.*

7) *Leave a couple of seconds at the end to fill in a random answer to the questions you haven't gotten around to completing. This isn't ideal but will likely happen to you in some sections just because of how time pressured this exam is. It's multiple choice so you might be lucky and get an answer right. You might as well - after all, that gamble might be the best thrill you get all summer!*

As a parent, the only bit of the UCAT I got involved with was the Situational Judgement section. My favourite game for a while was 'playing' situational judgement quizzes with Simon, Holly and my other daughter, Katie. Situational Judgement is the section of the UCAT test where they present the candidate with a tricky ethical situation and a choice of responses. The candidate has to decide which are 'very appropriate,' ' inappropriate but not awful,' or 'very inappropriate'. Everyone indulged my enthusiasm for the case studies, rolling their eyes when they thought I wasn't looking. When the others had called time on the 'game,' Holly and I used to compete to see who could get the most answers right in the allocated minutes. Holly quite enjoyed it because she always beat me.

At about this time, Holly, Katie and I went to see the musical, 'Waitress' in the West End for a birthday treat. One of the most entertaining musical numbers involves a highly lewd encounter between the protagonists: a doctor and his patient. While Katie and I tapped our feet to the rhythm of the music, Holly hissed in my ear, "Situational Judgement: very inappropriate!" and I felt my work was done.

In the Situational Judgement scenarios, it is usually obvious what is very inappropriate but the most appropriate form of action often requires careful thought which must include an understanding of NHS codes of ethics; this means it is not always the course of action that one instinctively might choose under the time pressure of the test. Situational judgement scores are not included in the final UCAT score but are assessed separately by the medical schools. Candidates are rated from the top, in band 1, to the bottom, in band 4. Most people when Holly applied scored in band 2, as she did. It was really important for Holly to spend time practising answering Situational Judgement tests because candidates whose scores are rated in band 4 may jeopardise everything. Many universities will not consider applications from candidates whose scores lie in band 4.

The Situational Judgement examples are also worth practising because they are helpful in getting candidates to understand ethical situations which might be discussed, or role played, in interview. Holly said she wished she'd been made to do a course in situational judgement before being let loose in hospital wards at the beginning of year 12. Of course, she learned to be tactful and discerning over the period of volunteering, but she admitted she was very naïve at first. There was one occasion when, from the side-lines, she witnessed an emergency procedure while shadowing a group of anaesthetists. She was so pleased to have learnt something new that when a woman marched up to her and said in an authoritative voice, "What are they doing?" she beamed at her and promptly answered, "He's having a tracheostomy." The woman's face crumpled. "Why are they doing that to my husband?" she said, and Holly realised too late the inappropriateness of her response.

In her defence, she immediately alerted a nurse to the woman's distress, explaining what she had blurted out. On another occasion, Holly was given the opportunity to watch a badly twisted testicle being removed in theatre. She still blushes at the memory of arriving in theatre and being asked why she was there. Flustered, she piped up, "I'm here for the penis." Eyebrows were raised. Still, when in one interview she was asked to recount an experience where she had made a mistake, at least she had a few to choose from.

HOLLY:

Ah, yes... thanks for reminding me... I had never wished to disappear and/or die as badly as I did in that moment...

On a more serious note, I would strongly recommend reading the Good Medical Practice guide and the Situational Judgement guidance in any of the UCAT textbooks before going in to do a work experience or volunteering placement.

Especially if you're 16 and completely new to it all. And slightly lacking in common sense... not that I would know anything about that...

Once Holly was committed to pursuing medicine, we gave her books[4] on studying for the UCAT and BMAT. She had a quick look and let out a few horrified gasps of laughter. Then she put the books out of sight towards the back of her dustiest bookshelf. During that first term in year 12, I added reminders about the aptitude tests to my list of indefatigable

---

[4] 700 BMAT Practice Questions (Campbell, Picard, 2016) and 1250 UKCAT Practice Questions (Picard, Tighlit et al, 2017)

nagging. "You ought to start working on your tests, Holly," I'd suggest, bruising my knuckles on her bedroom door to get her up early on a Sunday. "Just do one or two abstract reasoning tests a day," I'd say while she burrowed further under the duvet. Holly ignored my suggestions until the Christmas holidays when she tried doing a complete UCAT test. She came out with an average of 400 for most sections. She knew from researching the university admissions websites that she probably needed to get into the 600s to have a chance of an interview. She duly returned the books to the back of her bookshelf and refused to look at them again until her mock exams were over in the summer term. This sent me into paroxysms of anxiety but for all that I wailed to Mel about my fears, I understood that Holly was prioritising her A level work and her volunteering; time would prove that she was right to do so.

Throughout year 12, I advocated that Holly should take both the BMAT and the UCAT so that she would have a greater choice of universities to apply to but, unlike Holly, I didn't understand the differences between the tests. Although there is some overlap, Holly felt the BMAT would require her to recall her Physics GCSE whereas the UCAT would not. It was bad enough having to recall her Maths GCSE for both tests and she was acutely aware that there would be students applying who were studying Maths or Physics A level and that she had done less Physics than some candidates at GCSE. Holly hadn't taken separate sciences, but instead had chosen combined science; thus, whereas some students had three science GCSEs, she had only two. Furthermore, most universities require the UCAT and fewer want the BMAT. I knew that if she ruled out the BMAT she couldn't go to Brighton which I had been in favour of, selfishly thinking how easy it would be for me to get to; what a great excuse for a lovely trip to the seaside.

Without asking, Simon and I booked Holly on a day's course with Medic Portal, in preparation for both the UCAT and the BMAT. The UCAT course was in July after her end of year exams in year 12. She duly went along and said she found it useful but she refused to attend the BMAT course. This was booked for Easter and she just felt that she didn't have the time for it right then. We accepted this; with hindsight, we could see that we had been too impulsive about trying to help and should have taken more notice of what Holly wanted to do.

Holly booked the UCAT test for 8th August. She had eight weeks from the end of her year 12 exams to focus on revising for the UCAT. On the 9th we were leaving on a plane for our annual two week holiday. I thought Holly should have used the two weeks' holiday to carry on revising, but her father thought she should have a total break while on holiday and he and Holly agreed on the date. In fact, Holly had quietly planned to use the two weeks while on holiday to finish her EPQ essay. Her lap-top and textbooks were duly packed for the holiday and Simon took her up on the train to Holborn where she was booked into the Pearson test centre to sit her exam.

We chose the Pearson test centre at Holborn because we knew it. Firstly, Simon had done an exam at the centre a couple of years earlier, and, secondly, my friend's nephew had done his UCAT there. This was the lad who had scored an average over 700 in his UCAT and had got into Exeter. In addition, this lad had recently done his driving test theory exam in the centre at Watford, our nearest one, and he had been dismayed at how noisy it had been. He had met a candidate in tears outside who had just sat her UCAT. The computers had crashed in the middle of it and she had not done as well as she had hoped. That anecdote put us off Watford and we were keen to book Holborn well in advance of the date because we knew it would be well organised and quiet.

Holly's test was late morning. She was keen to be as alert as possible. On some insane level her father thought it would be a good idea to buy her two espressos before she went in. Two espressos? For a teenager who hardly touched coffee? Holly handed in her passport with hands shaking like a pneumatic drill from rocketing, caffeine-fuelled adrenalin. She predicted that if she didn't hit the 600s – ideally an average of 650 she would be at a massive disadvantage in the applicant selection process. The test is done on a computer screen and each section is timed. Once your time is up for that section you cannot go back to answer any questions you may have missed at the end. There is a calculator facility on screen and there is a whiteboard tablet for working out sums. The on-screen calculator is slow and tricky to use which is why it is important to sharpen up your mental maths and practise on UCAT's simulator website. The first section was verbal reasoning which was Holly's strongest section. When practising the test, she had scored in the 700s for this, even once getting 800. It was probably just as well that her strongest was first because, initially, her hand was trembling so much that she couldn't control the mouse and lost precious seconds fumbling about trying to click on the right answer.

 In addition to UCAT and BMAT practice books, YouTube. and past papers, make sure you use the UCAT simulator as the real on-screen calculator is clunky and needs getting used to.

Despite this, the test went really well. The beauty of the UCAT, unlike the BMAT, is that you get your score immediately. Holly had scored a total of 2670, or an average of 667 across the four sections. At this point we still didn't know where she would come in terms of deciles. This information comes later and we had already decided which universities to apply to by then. It is important how the cohort does but you cannot know how you compare with those who have applied to your specific choices. Each university ranks their students according to the calibre of those who apply. Holly's score was relevant only to the other applicants for Cardiff, Sheffield, Birmingham and Hull/York. Perhaps this is why universities don't like publishing historical cut off scores, as the cut off scores for choosing applicants will vary from year to year. It is clear that, in most cases, the BMAT and UCAT scores are extremely important in determining whether or not you get an interview. Holly's experience would suggest that it is well worth revising for the aptitude tests. (Holly made it into the 7th decile nationally, putting her in the top 30% which was great, although we didn't know if the people applying to her choice of universities would be representative of the full range.)

Holly started off revising intermittently with the textbooks and supplementing this with an online testing course and YouTube videos. She realised that testing herself online was more effective and significant than using the textbooks we had bought her because practising on-line replicated the demands of the test. She needed to be able to use a calculator on screen and had to be adept at manoeuvring through the test at speed. The medics who post advice on how to approach the sections of the UCAT test on YouTube were particularly helpful to her. She spent so much time gazing at the screen, listening to the advice of Kharma Medic that her sister made her a t-shirt with his face on it. I hope he won't be disturbed to know that throughout her A levels it was her favourite to sleep in. There is no doubt that Holly's revision paid off. She may not have done it all year, as I had hoped, but she spent at least six weeks revising for it for several hours a day and it was important that she did. There is no point getting excellent predicted grades and a list of voluntary placements as long as your arm if you mess up the aptitude test. You can sit it only once a year and, for most universities, your application success largely depends on getting a good score.

Don't underestimate the demands of the aptitude tests or their significance in getting an interview. Try to use as many practice book resources you can afford, and particularly view advice from medics on YouTube. In the last couple of weeks, prior to the test, do online exam simulations.

And finally, try to book a quiet and efficient test centre – ask your teachers or research your nearest test centres using social media or online reviews.

Chapter 5

Choosing Universities

Initially, we thought of those universities which I had randomly selected before Holly embarked on her sixth form subjects and who had all assured me that Fine Art was a perfectly viable third A level.

Hull/York was also appealing because it had created 70 extra places for medicine, and we knew they took into account the EPQ qualification. We knew it was a split campus and that students were randomly allocated Hull or York. We thought York would be an attractive place to live, so we didn't need to visit it, and thought we could just go to the open day at Hull to check if Holly would be happy there. Personally, I was happy with her going to Hull, fantasizing about visiting the library where the poet Philip Larkin once worked. This proved less of a pull for Holly, although she enjoyed quoting "This be the Verse" at me whenever I alluded to it.

We chose Cardiff because it put less emphasis on UCAT and more on other elements of the application, such as GCSEs and personal statement, and a friend's daughter had gone there and loved it. I'm also Welsh, so Holly had an affinity with Wales and South Wales was a familiar destination for her.

We considered Barts Medical School and went to the open day at Queen Mary's. The points system meant that while the EPQ would be counted, candidates who had a grade 6 or above in dance and musical instruments would also gain points. It was apparent that Holly's grade 1 in ballet and piano wouldn't really float their boats.

We ended up putting Sheffield down because Holly's friend's sister recommended it and when we rang them to check, they were happy with Fine Art as an A level. They were part of the Russell group and there was nothing to suggest that Holly wouldn't get an interview. We did look at league tables such as the Guardian university Guide and Simon made another spreadsheet comparing different rating systems. He was of the view that there wasn't much between the medical schools, despite the fact that universities did move up and down year on year, perhaps according to cohort responses. It was difficult to decide how reliable the league tables were. However, Sheffield did stand out for year on year having significantly high student satisfaction and this was a big factor in our encouraging Holly to apply there.

We weren't sure whether to put Birmingham or UEA as the other choice. Birmingham has an on-line algorithm where you put in your predicted grades and your UCAT score and they tell you whether or not you are likely to be offered an interview. Holly put in 3 starred A predictions and her average UCAT of 667 and got a positive response. We compared the ratio of applicants to interviews and then the ratio of interviewees to offers and decided that we would plump for Birmingham over UEA. The daughter of one of Holly's favourite teachers had recently finished training at Birmingham and had loved it. Birmingham also counted academic qualifications and predictions highly weighting them against the UCAT 60: 40. This would work in Holly's favour. So, ultimately it was this combination of factual research and anecdotal information that led to our four choices.

Brighton had been keen to consider a student whose third subject was Art but sadly, my fantasy sea-view visits were out of the picture once Holly decided not to sit the BMAT.

Her final four choices of Cardiff, Birmingham, Sheffield and Hull /York (HYMS) were ultimately a solid selection. They were all fairly mid-ranging on the league tables and thus in terms of popularity they weren't the trickiest to get into. Holly said that as long as she could study medicine, there was nowhere she would be unhappy to go. Of course, with these four choices, it was still going to be incredibly competitive but perhaps she had given herself a better chance by not putting down the top four universities in the league tables for that year and - by ignoring my advice - limiting herself to preparing for one aptitude test only.

Open Days

Holly could take only two days out of school for open days but could go to as many as she liked in her holidays and at weekends. This was all very well, but the reality was that she just didn't have the time to visit places while juggling all of the other demands on her time: volunteering, visiting Art galleries for Art A level, and doing her day-to-day homework; plus, revision for the end of year exams on which her predicted grades would depend.

Her school had put on a fantastic UCAS fair in the spring term of year 12 that was open to the whole community and at which she was able to talk to representatives from a whole range of universities. Holly had been talking to friends and ex-students about their experiences and she looked at on-line virtual tours of universities.

Before she made her choices she visited Cardiff, Hull, Queen Mary, Brighton, Birmingham and Sheffield, to get a feel for the course and the places. Cardiff and Hull/York arranged brilliant open days which were slickly organised. Hull/York arranged accommodation in student halls of residence and even reimbursed us for a percentage of our travel costs. The campus was appealing at Hull and Holly's only complaint was that the showers in the students' rooms were too powerful!

Cardiff's Open Day clearly enthused Holly; she was fizzing with excitement after a day of independence from parental influence (adults were separated from the students all day and taken to their own lectures) and an understanding of what Cardiff had to offer.

Holly and Simon took a train to Sheffield and Birmingham on one of the open days in September. Holly had already put her choices down so they just made a whistle-stop tour to talk to medical students about the course and get a flavour of the campus in Birmingham's case and some sense of the student union in Sheffield's, cramming it into one exhausting day. Possibly, when it came down to it, the fact that Holly chose Cardiff had quite a lot to do with her open day experience and the timing of it. Having said that, medicine is not like Law, where the institute where you study has a bearing on whether or not you go further in terms of becoming a fully-fledged lawyer. We were certainly of the view that a good place to study medicine is anywhere that is willing to offer you a place.

Consequently, we were keen to put down places that she had the best chance of getting an offer from; although, we suggested to Holly that she rule out Scotland and Ireland as too far away for ease of travel. Our parental role was important at this point. Holly had a shocking knowledge of British geography before she applied to university; until she went to Sheffield's open day, she thought the Peak district was in Cornwall!

Visit the universities on open days when you can speak to medical students, and if there's a choice of dates go early as possible. Be prepared to give up time again later in Year 13 to attend offer-holder open days, which will be more focused on you and will definitely help inform your UCAS strategy.

The Fifth Choice

Holly's school were insistent that their medics all put down a fifth choice. You can choose only four options for medicine and can leave the fifth blank, but if a candidate doesn't get an offer for medicine, even if their strategy is to re-apply, they will feel less downhearted if they have an offer for something. This 'something' is usually Bio-med as it can be another route to get into medicine. Most places will allow a certain percentage of their highest achieving Bio-med students to move across to Medicine after the first year – though you do still have to do the relevant aptitude test again. Holly had decided that she would take a gap year and reapply rather than go down that route but she followed her school's advice and duly informed me that she'd put down Bio-med at Bristol which required 3 A grades. I was a bit shocked that she hadn't discussed this decision with me but I didn't let on, as the deed was done. It wasn't until after she received an offer from them that I asked her why she'd chosen this particular university, prestigious as it was. At the time, she was skipping about the kitchen with a little card from Bristol congratulating her on her offer, which was a cute touch on their part. I was labouring over the chopping board, making dinner.

"Well," she said, "I enjoyed talking to the dude with piercings all over his face about his experiences as a medic and at least I'd been to the open day."

"Er…wasn't that Brighton?" I said.

"Oh yeah," she said with a dawning grin. "I keep getting them mixed up!"

Then she waltzed back out of the kitchen, leaving me jabbing my knife hard at the onions.

Weighing up the differences between Universities

It was really important to look up the information for each course on each university's admissions website and make notes so that we could clearly see the differences between them. Simon made a spreadsheet comparing all the medical schools in terms of entrance requirements, interview style, teaching methods, and applicant success ratios. As we got more information (and Holly's UCAT scores) we gradually filtered out universities to leave a shortlist. I've included a sample of our spreadsheet with the caveat that things may change slightly, year on year. Holly didn't have time to put together this analysis and so I think it was a good thing that Simon did this for her.

HOLLY:

> *This was an amazing thing my Dad did for me! Being strategic when choosing what you put down for Medicine is so important and there's so much information to look at regarding each University's unique entry requirements.*
>
> *Without this spreadsheet and having a conversation with my parents where they helped me evaluate the likelihood of my success at attaining an interview at each one, I doubt I would have been able to secure all four invitations to interview. It will take a huge weight off your med kid if you can put together a spreadsheet of info for them!*

The spreadsheet image on the next page is just a small extract of the full sheet, just to illustrate how we laid it out, and colour-coded scores or comments on how favourable the requirements were to Holly's chances. For our younger daughter we have added columns like distance from home and driving or train travel time. If you'd like a copy of Holly's med school selection spreadsheet, please email us at: medschool@leasidebooks.com

University	GCSE Requirements	GCSE Holly	A levels required	A-level grades required	A-levels Holly	Test	Use of UCAT
Cardiff	All applicants must achieve the minimum requirements at GCSE. Applicants will receive a score based on their best nine GCSEs. This score will include the following subjects: English Language - 6 (B); At least one of Mathematics or Numeracy - 6 (B); Science - Either; 66 or BB in Science and Additional Science (formerly Double Award Science) or equivalent or 66 (BB) in Chemistry and Biology. Or, 66 (BB) in Core Science and one of Additional Science or further Additional Science. Other subjects not stated above, to make a total of nine, at a minimum of grade B.	OK	Chemistry and Biology.	AAA	OK. 3rd A-level required but not specified.	UKCAT	Cardiff does not have a minimum threshold score for the UKCAT, however, the UKCAT score may be used as part of the assessment procedure or in borderline cases. Requirements for 2020 entry will be available in August 2019.
Bristol	Advanced numeracy requirement (A in GCSE Maths or equivalent) and Standard literacy requirement (C in GCSE English or equivalent).	OK	Chemistry and either Biology, Physics or Maths.	AAA or lower with EPQ	OK. 3rd A-level required but not specified.	UKCAT	The weightings of your application are as follows: GCSE 15%, A-level 15%, Personal statement 50%, UKCAT 20%. Using data from 2017/18 cycle, applicants with a UKCAT score of 2660 or above would have been issued with an invitation to interview had we been solely using UKCAT for selection. Where applicants choose to offer the Extended Project alongside A-levels, we may make two alternative offers: one of which involves success in the Extended Project
UCL	All UK candidates, or those who have received their secondary education in the UK, must offer GCSE (or IGCSE, O-level, IB or EB equivalent) at grade B or above in both English Language and Mathematics. For candidates taking the new style of GCSEs with numerical outcomes rather than letter grades, the requirement is for a score of 6 in both English Language and Mathematics. UCL expects all UK applicants to offer a Modern Foreign Language (not including Ancient Greek, Biblical Hebrew or Latin) at GCSE grade C or equivalent (the requirement for the new style of GCSEs with numerical outcomes will be score of 5).	No - require a foreign language	Chemistry and Biology. The third subject is the student's own choice.	A*AA	OK. 3rd may be anything	BMAT	

The worksheet structure was as below, but of course you can adapt it as you wish.

Column heading	Notes
University	
GCSE Requirements	From Medical School admissions website
GCSE Holly	How do the student's GCSE's match the requirements?
A-level requirements	From Medical School admissions website
A-level grades required	From Medical School admissions website
A-levels Holly	How do the student's A-levels match – especially for the third A-level?
Test	UCAT or BMAT
Use of UCAT	How heavily does the med school rely on UCAT (or BMAT) compared to other criteria?
Learning Style	Integrated / Case Based / Problem Based / Traditional etc.
Interview Style	MMI or Traditional
Applicant Success Rate	Scores from your preferred newspaper or guidebook
Student-Staff ratio	
Money spent per student	
Student satisfaction	
Personal choice	Towards the end of your online investigations (and after your open day visits) enter a rough ranking of preference
Website	Cut and paste the med school admissions web address for easy reference

The admissions websites for each university will give you and your child a lot of important information. A lot of questions will be answered by reading all on-line information carefully. However, if you have specific questions regarding their approach which aren't answered on their website, you can email or ring them. In my experience, admissions teams respond immediately and are really helpful. If you have a question that they are unable to answer, you can apply for an FOI (Freedom of Information) regarding your question.

From what I can tell from following threads in The Student Room, people sometimes make FOI requests when they want facts or statistics about the selection process for a particular year from a specific university. But really, the published statistics will give you a good guide, and of course the actual cut-off scores or deciles will vary every year anyway.

Holly was obviously keen to look at the way the courses were structured and the differences in the way she would be taught. Simon and I had no input on that element because only Holly could discern what was going to appeal to her. We were interested to hear how keen she was on dissection and on small group learning which both excited and daunted her. There were some differences in the sizes of the cohorts and in the way the students were taught at Holly's four choices and this had some bearing on the ultimate decision that she made to go to Cardiff.

This may sound obvious, but the primary driver for your four UCAS choices must be the four universities that are most likely to offer you an interview, based on your analysis of how they assess applications and your relative strengths. Other preferences of location and even Open Day performance can be applied as 'tie breakers' – but you need those interviews first!

At open days ask about differences in course structure, placement locations and placement demands, and of course facilities for studying, living, and socialising!

Take into consideration that hospital placements can vary greatly, and students may be required to relocate to other cities or towns for short periods of the course. For example, Cardiff students have placements in Bangor or Rhyl, and UEA have placements in Great Yarmouth, amongst others. Placement durations can vary according to the curriculum at different institutions.

Chapter 6

The Personal Statement

Some universities don't even look at the personal statement before selecting for interview, others do, and some use it as part of the MMI (Multiple Mini Interviews). Even if personal statements are not given significant weighting, they are still worth doing well because the information is going to have a bearing on what the candidate talks about at interview. When Holly sat down to write her first draft for her personal statement, it was the first time she had tried fully to articulate reflections on her volunteering experience.

I was surprised how few words were allowed in the personal statement. The limit is given in the form of characters / letters. The number of characters is 4000. The first thing Holly needed to consider was how many elements of voluntary work she could get into her personal statement, bearing in mind that she couldn't just list what she had done. She had to reflect upon the value of each experience, exploring as succinctly as possible what she had gained from it. Holly was given advice from school but there is also plenty of advice to be had from online sources like The Student Room and from Medic Portal which are free to access.

Holly's personal statement began with an interest in her subjects and why she wanted to do medicine. Having worried that Fine Art, being a largely practical A level might not be considered 'rigorous' enough as a third A level for some admissions tutors, Holly addressed it at the outset to make a virtue of it. Perhaps it could make her stand out from the students who were following a more traditional path. Holly wrote many drafts of her personal statement finding that she had to keep editing what she wanted to say because she didn't have the space to explain how academically curious she was, how enthusiastic about applying herself to the course and how affected she was by experiences she'd had while volunteering. Obviously, she needed to write it herself and so my input was largely just to check for typos, and occasionally to help rephrase a sentence so that it took up fewer words. Her teachers also checked it through for her and gave her advice on clarity and the development of her points. Inevitably, Holly was far more willing to listen to them than to me, but fundamentally, she had to decide for herself what to include and how to say it. She read other people's statements and that gave her a good idea of the expectations.

Holly's personal statement is reproduced below. I have analysed its strengths, but I am not suggesting it is a perfect statement by any means. Everyone's will be different according to their subjective experience. Holly's is reproduced with her kind permission, just as an example.

Read other people's Personal Statements and follow the format (not the content!) that other successful applicants have used.

Your aim is to make your Personal Statement clear and easy to read, so the time-pressed Med School reviewer can tick off their requirements without hunting through a lot of waffle.

Holly's Personal Statement

"As an A Level Art student, I interpret the sitter holistically when painting a portrait. I analyse gestures and expressions whilst building trust. During my work experience I was struck by the parallels between this process and that of the doctor who must make assessments sensitively and humanely, recognising the patient as an individual, not just a diagnosis waiting to be solved. **(Links approaches taken in the study of Fine Art to a doctor's ethos)**

My role in the Empathy Project has shown I have insight and resilience. Empathy is a Youth Connections scheme based at the Lister Hospital. Peer supporters, selected through interview, chat to teenagers presenting at A&E, signposting them to mental health services where suitable. A Mental Health First Aid Course helped me to communicate appropriately with a CAMHS patient. I learnt the importance of building a trusting and safe environment, when talking about sensitive issues such as social anxiety. I remained composed despite being moved by the experiences described. **(Shows evidence of resilience, empathy, and communication skills)**

I was nominated for a Stevenage Borough Council award by Youth Connections for using my initiative and having moved beyond my 'comfort zone in terms of approaching patients and holding meaningful conversations with them.' These skills were further enhanced during five days at Rennie Grove Hospice where I listened to patients and joined in with therapeutic games. Shadowing a Diabetes Specialist Nurse in a clinic taught me the importance of strict diabetes monitoring. I went on to volunteer for weekly 3 hour shifts at the Lister for 3 months, on the Renal Ward where many Type 2 Diabetics received dialysis. I also witnessed a nephrectomy in theatre (and held the diseased kidney!) so the significance of early intervention was impressed upon me. Some of the renal patients were lower limb amputees suffering from Phantom

Limb Pain. This motivated me to focus my EPQ on prosthetic limbs, exploring how current advances restore independence and improve quality of life. **(Reflecting on what she learnt from her shadowing and volunteering, linking it to her enthusiasm for independent learning)**

The teamwork and camaraderie of multi-disciplinary-teams at the Lister was just as impressive as that seen in my week at the Metabolic Department at Great Ormond Street Hospital. Dieticians, play specialists, metabolic nurses and paediatricians needed to work together to ensure that patients with complex metabolic diseases such as PKU were treated correctly. Effective communication is clearly a central skill and one which I exhibit in my roles as Careers Prefect, leader of the lower school book club, and a St John Ambulance cadet. A day shadowing a Trust CEO gave me some insight into management concerns. A meeting tackling harassment of nurses made me aware of the scope and value of these roles. While observing a team of ICU Anaesthetists for an afternoon, a consultant told me how important it was to be 'judgement aware'; to know the limits of one's skills and consider levels of fatigue when deciding to do a procedure. I manage my workload effectively to avoid fatigue and stress, improving through tenacity and diligence. This was recognised through my Academic Award for Biology. **(Further evidence of reflection and links made between the qualities displayed by health professionals such as teamwork, effective communication, understanding one's limitations, and evidence of these qualities in her own life)**

Studying Chemistry has enabled me to hone my planning and problem-solving skills. Biology deepens my curiosity regarding anatomy; learning about the cerebrum was especially interesting. My enthusiasm for science is matched by my love of literature and art which gives me both solace and breadth to my view of the world, its problems and its potential. This year, for Fine Art, I intend to research neurological diseases such as dementia and present what I have learnt in a creative medium. Books like 'Still Alice' and 'Somebody I Used to Know' have supplemented this interest. My varied work experience has given me a greater understanding of medical fields, cementing my belief that I would thrive as a medic. I am excited by the possibility of fulfilling my vocation."

(The final paragraph sums up elements of her A levels that have interested her and are relevant to the course she is applying for. She mentions relevant wider reading, which, like the EPQ show evidence of enthusiasm and interest which move beyond the curriculum. Her final comments reinforce the sense of her as an enthusiastic and resolute candidate with some awareness of the demands of medical fields.)

Chapter 7

The Interviews

Holly clicked 'send' with the fatalism of a naval officer authorising the release of a nuclear missile, sending off her UCAS form a week or so before the deadline in early October. All we could do now was cross our fingers that she had chosen wisely and would get an interview at least one of her four choices. We knew that interviews could happen from November through to February in year 13 and, indeed, this is what happened. Throughout the autumn term of year 13 the school were excellent at bringing in previous students and parents with a background in Medicine to come and talk to the students and to conduct mock interviews; no doubt this helped a lot.

Without asking her we had also booked Holly on an MMI day through Medic Portal way back in January of year 12. According to Holly she was the only one there who wasn't facing an interview imminently and with hindsight she had more sympathy for the haunted looks and gravitas of her peers on that day. At first, she was cross with us for arranging an MMI day when she felt she hadn't had enough experience of her A level subjects, volunteering or preparation time. She had a point, in that she was limited in what she could draw on to answer questions, but it had value. She gained an understanding of how the interviews worked, in that you move from mini interview panel to mini interview panel, spending several minutes at each station with a few minutes in between to read through the questions or tasks which lie at each station.

At each station, during the practice day, students were given immediate feedback. Holly's light-hearted approach to greeting a stranger in her role-play task had the interviewers bursting out laughing at one station and, at another, her misinterpretation of a question on ethics left the interviewer repeating the question to her, in bewilderment, three times. Holly related these experiences to me afterwards in good spirits. At this point she wasn't worried; after all, the real interviews were a long way off and she had enjoyed the day. I, on the other hand, spent a lot of time muttering while filling the dishwasher and pairing socks, imagining myself being interviewed in this intense manner, mouthing the answers I would give, my stomach flipping over at the thought of MMIs; memories of spectacularly cocking up a few interviews in my own career surged up, threatening to drown all reason. I just had to stop ruminating and remind myself that she might be my daughter, but she wasn't me; if she could only get an interview, with enough preparation, she would probably be all right.

 Medic Portal's MMI Day is excellent preparation. To get the most out of it, it helps to have some volunteering or shadowing experience under your belt first so you can practise describing learning points or self-reflection during the mini-interviews.

HOLLY:

The Medic Portal's MMI Course was amazing in that it was such an accurate imitation of the structure of the more traditional MMI interviews- so it was particularly good practice for Cardiff and Birmingham.

By more traditional I mean that if you've been told that you are doing an MMI circuit of approximately 8 stations lasting around 6-8 minutes each, then this MMI Portal will be invaluable for you. Hull/ York added more frills to the interview structure by telling us they would include a mystery task, a roleplay which was on a separate floor, a group PBL style discussion, ending with 2 MMI stations... That's what I would call a non-traditional MMI format.

The Medic Portal course is great preparation because you get to do around 20 stations, so it's pretty intense - more intense than an actual MMI circuit I would argue - although there's less pressure to perform at your best in this practice round. The fact that you're in a big hall where you rotate to each MMI cubicle, enclosed usually by only a thin curtain, with everybody talking at once, really tests your concentration and endurance. It perfectly encapsulates the weird, stressful ambience of the MMI circuit which is something that is really hard to mimic with your friends and family when you are forcing them to help you prepare for an MMI.

You get to rotate with another person too. You do one station and then they do the next, so you get to see how they answer questions which can be reassuring (everybody waffles) and makes the day a lot more fun! I should do it again just so I get another buddy - nothing brings people together like shared trauma.

(Sadly, in a real MMI circuit you don't get a free friend or the break between stations and most people just exchange scared but sympathetic glances as they pass each other).

As you've already read, I did this MMI circuit right back at the start of year 12, which is not ideal. I didn't treat it as a serious interview and didn't do any preparation for it at all which meant I didn't feel the full benefits from it in terms of getting more specific feedback from my interviewers. My advice would be to try to treat it as seriously as you can and do it when your interview is perhaps a month or two away. This way you have time to improve on the constructive feedback you've been given for your almost-polished performance.

Holly's first interview invitation was from Cardiff, swiftly followed by one from Sheffield. Hot on their heels came an invitation from Hull/York. Each time she got an interview invitation, Holly and I roared with joy and indulged ourselves with a dance to Pharrell Williams around the kitchen, our pulses racing at the unexpected success! This was tempered by the knowledge that all bets were off and that from this point nothing else mattered except the interview itself. Those assessing her would not be the same people who had decided she was worth interviewing, they would not have seen her UCAS application with its list of qualifications and the glowing reference. They would not have read her personal statement and so they would know nothing about her. Holly would be relying on her initiative to convey to different interviewers at each station, in just a handful of minutes, why she was worth choosing out of all these other talented candidates. In the interview she would be starting from scratch.

HOLLY:

Some of the queries I've had so far about the MMI interviews from new year 12s, are the same questions I had right at the beginning. These were usually along the lines of: how much of your personal statement will they ask you about? Will I have to know everything about this book I barely read but namedropped in my personal statement? Are they going to grill me on the diagnosis and treatment for this niche disease I mentioned?

The answer is no! Don't stress about the personal statement for MMIs!

I think this is a common misconception about the MMIs that I really want to tattoo onto every aspiring medic's cerebrum. It is solely up to you to bring up the volunteering experience anecdotes, the hobbies, the EPQ and up to you as to how much detail you describe it in. Everything you've stuffed into that personal statement can totally be used in an MMI but you have to apply it appropriately to the questions asked. The questions will generally be pretty open- ended and the interviewers will want you to use the work experience, research etc as evidence to back up your arguments. But ultimately none of those interviewers will have read your statement- they won't be able to turn that lovingly crafted essay into a pop quiz.

*(**Disclaimer**: If you are a clever cookie applying to Oxbridge or another university doing panel interviews then, to my knowledge, they do sometimes look at personal statements and so my above reassurance does not apply).*

That said, don't completely turn your back on your personal statement and flush the pages of The Epigenetic Revolution down the loo. As hated as the personal statement is, it has probably really helped you summarise all that work experience/volunteering you've done and has made you reflect on what you've learnt. It might also be helpful to be able to concisely talk about that research you've done on x disease and the fancy books you've read as you may well want to use it to answer a question.

If nothing else, use the personal statement as a starting point to really delve into each volunteering placement and then, if you haven't been able to already, you will begin to be able to articulate the answer to that dreaded question: why do you want to do Medicine?

"Why do you want to do medicine?" can leave you vaguely waffling about helping people – not a solid response in an interview or a Personal Statement. Instead think about one of a doctor's behaviours or functions that really impresses or interests you. Then refer to a real, specific instance when you saw that behaviour in action, and how it made you feel. Perhaps this happened during your volunteering, or was a memorable event when you, or family, or friends were being treated in a healthcare setting.

Holly could choose the date and time for her interview according to the dates on offer, but it was on a first come first served basis. She had only a matter of weeks before her first interview. She was a bit hesitant, trying to work out the day that would disrupt schoolwork least, so by the time we agreed a date it was already fully booked. She ended up having to do the first two interviews only 7 days apart in November.

She made her decision more quickly the next time and was able to choose a bigger gap between Sheffield and Hull/York which was in late December. In the first rush of excitement for Cardiff and Sheffield, Holly didn't notice that at the end of the invitations there was crucial information on documents she needed to bring to identify who she was (passport or provisional driving licence) and some key information on the way the MMIs would be structured and where they would be held. Luckily, on further scrutiny a few days later, she noticed the extra stuff at the end of the document. This was crucial for the Sheffield interview as the invitation had come with a list of questions!

Holly

Yes, please scroll down to the end of the email on your interview invitation for vital information! What kind of fool would forget to do that… ahem?

The amount of information you get given about your MMI will vary depending on the university. For example, for Cardiff all I got told about the actual interview in the invitation was that it was going to last 80 minutes. Whereas in Hull/York there was a video sent along with the email which outlined how many stations there were, what each station was going to contain through use of vague terms (e. g a roleplay station, a group task, a mystery task, two standard MMI stations) and how long the stations would last. Birmingham also told us roughly what kind of stations there would be, how many and how long each station would last. Sheffield went one step further in terms of transparency by giving us the exact questions beforehand, some of which required a little research (although the follow up questions were new, fresh and minty).

Interview Preparation

Holly spent a great deal of time preparing for the interviews (probably to the detriment of her mock examination preparation). Even so, she came away from each interview convinced that she hadn't done well enough. Holly's Dad was very reassured by the tutor who spoke to parents at the Sheffield interview day. He told everyone that inevitably their child will come out of the interview obsessing over one or two things that went wrong. He said the important thing to remember is that EVERYONE does one or two things wrong and that they don't need to get upset about it. Holly was no different. In each post- mortem she could think of things she'd done 'wrong', though clearly no-one is going to give the perfect interview. Despite her misgivings, her preparation paid off.

HOLLY:

Okay, so in order to prepare for these interviews you have to get into the mindset of Danny Ocean in "Ocean's Eleven". You, sir, are planning the biggest heist yet but before you get the bags of cash and Julia Roberts, (a.k.a. your offers for med school), so you are going to need some serious preparation. (Sadly, you don't get to do this with Brad Pitt.)

So, before you can go to the Bellagio, you have got to have done some reflection in order to sift out those golden, personal anecdotes from your work experience, school and extracurriculars. Typically, you will want ones that display your communication skills, leadership skills, your teamwork skills, your empathy, your resilience, your interest in problem solving and your intellectual curiosity. In most of the MMIs I sat there was an emphasis on the importance of having insight and an awareness of your own limitations and judgement. When reflecting on your past year make sure to acknowledge your failures and mistakes and how you have been active in trying to improve yourself and your behaviour as a result of this reflection.

Ideally, you also want to have anecdotes from your shadowing/ volunteering experience where you saw healthcare staff who also exhibited the skills I listed above. This shows an understanding of what it's like to work in a healthcare setting. Try to have around 10 anecdotes up your sleeve that you know really well which cater to each of these areas, often an anecdote will be able to show more than just one of these skills which is really neat.

When practising these answers first write down what you want to say, memorise it briefly and then try to apply the answer to a question. Don't memorise it word for word otherwise you might get into the habit of reeling off a scripted, robotic-sounding answer. On the other hand, you need to be good at formulating your points succinctly and cogently so that you can say all the things you need to get across in a two minute answer.

Do think long and hard about answering the 'Why medicine? Why this course? This uni? This town?' questions as truthfully and as enthusiastically as you can. In some shape or form this ground is bound to be covered. There is no excuse for not having thought through really strong answers to these obvious and key questions. After all, they need to know that if they pick you, you are going to be happy and committed to their course, in their location.

Spend a good few months practising interview questions with anyone you can get your hands on (with their consent). And I mean anyone. Teachers, family, friends and perhaps, at a push, siblings. Bonus points for persuading healthcare professionals and strangers to interview you. If you're lucky enough to have a school that organises medical professionals to come to interview you then make sure you go to those meetings. You will be interviewed by many medical professionals in your MMIs so you need to be able to perform well in front of people you know you can't talk nonsense to. It will be nerve-wracking but helpful in the long run. You want to get comfortable with being interviewed by people you are completely unfamiliar with, people who know nothing about your voluntary experience; basically, people who know nothing about you at all. Try to do everything to mirror the real MMI situation.

Relatively consistent and regular interview practice is invaluable and in reality, will likely be with people you are familiar with. Try and get your buddies to help you out at lunchtimes by asking you some MMI questions. There are a huge number of questions with exemplar answers online on platforms like Medic Portal, Blackstone tutors and can also be found in the beautiful 'Medical School Interviews' book by ISC Medical.

The 'Medical School Interviews' book by ISC Medical is an incredible resource for MMIs and you can find my full review of it in the Appendix. In the 2ⁿᵈ Edition I used there were over 150 questions split into 5 categories: questions on motivation and interest in medical issues, questions on the course and the Medical School, questions on interpersonal skills and personal insight, questions testing critical thinking and wacky questions. My advice would be to read the first few pages of each chapter, look at the advice, tips and the exemplar responses and then save the rest for someone else to test you on. Or if no one is around and you just want to party solo, read the question and record yourself giving the answer. Listen back to it and see if you covered all the key points offered in the book.

It can be really nice to practise with fellow aspiring medics as you can see the strengths and weaknesses in each other's answers and gain constructive criticism. If you have a Medsoc in 6ᵗʰ form devote some sessions to purely MMI type interview stations. If your Medsoc is really organised perhaps they will set up a little lunchtime circuit with generous staff acting as your interviewers.

I can confess that my MMI practice wasn't particularly routine and regular; my method was pretty much just 'try to do it whenever you have spare time'. Better time management probably would have enabled me to do more practice. Try to organise at least an hour a day where you are completely absorbed in MMI practice for about 2 months before your first interview. My parents were really great at testing me as often as possible and weren't afraid of giving me feedback, sometimes constructive, sometimes insulting... It's also understandable if you can't get your friends to practice with you 24/7 because at the end of the day, you probably don't want them to hate you.

If you're smart you will have been reading up on everything NHS related in the news since the end of Year 11. Don't panic if you haven't- I admit I just glanced at the news every couple of months to check up on the NHS and didn't really absorb it into my long-term memory. But when your interview is a month away you really need to start paying attention to all the scandals and reforms that occurred in the last couple of years. It can be a lot to remember but it's really helpful to have a widespread knowledge of everything related to medical news, including advances in medical research. Usually, the hot topics will be pretty obvious but they can also be found summed up on Medic portal. I would encourage you to pay attention to the big changes in healthcare that have recently been proposed or put in action in the year you are sitting your interviews.

I hope these tips help. Oh, and remember to breathe. Good luck Mr. Ocean!

What Holly told me after the interviews

All four interviews followed fairly similar MMI formats. Each was a mixture of questions on motivation to be a doctor, personal and academic interests, understanding of the codes and ethics of the medical profession and the NHS, an awareness of current issues affecting medicine and the NHS. Cardiff and Birmingham had some stations dedicated to testing mental Maths and all but Cardiff had a role play element. Holly, having had her ability in Maths undermined by year 6 teachers, was never very confident in Maths (Yep! I'm still bitter!) and so she dreaded the Maths element of the interviews. She was also aware that many students would have taken Maths A level, instead of gladly waving it goodbye at GCSE. On the other hand, she was lucky that she has always been very good at acting and although she regarded herself as socially awkward this is all relative. In fact, the majority of the MMI stations played to her strengths; she was good at recounting anecdotal experiences and good at role play. In the days before her interviews I enjoyed indulging my hypochondria by taking on the patient's role and acting out a five minute conversation with her. Usually, it seems, the candidate is asked only to be themselves in these role plays but they are given an objective and being observed on their approach so this is not a natural situation and thus, it is a performance.

Holly had got a lot better at addressing a stranger since that MMI practice day almost a year earlier, because she had been volunteering so much and because we practised how she would accost someone in the role play part of the interview. There was a world of difference between the naïve 16 year old starting her A levels and the competent 18 year old she had become by her final interview. In each MMI, body language, eye contact and empathetic facial expression were probably as important as what she said. She was good at listening as well as asking tactful, open ended questions which would have helped in the role play scenario. On the day, it seemed what was also being tested was common sense and an honest awareness of one's limitations.

At **Cardiff** there was an ice- breaker activity. It started with a member of staff asking for interesting facts. Having recently acquired a love of Robert de Niro, Holly reeled off a few facts about the Gambino Mafia. Then everyone else gave facts about the human body. Holly felt this didn't bode well. Luckily, she wasn't being assessed on this workshop so she needn't have worried (although afterwards, on the way out, she happened to pass the tutor in charge of the ice-breaker, who admitted her unexpected answer had made them chuckle).

One of the key challenges for Holly was how noisy the MMIs were. Everyone was in the same room and talking at the same time and this was quite distracting. Holly felt annoyed with herself that at one station she didn't take on board the instructions. They were told to read the questions through to the end before answering but she just plunged in headlong. She then realised that the last question had significantly more marks attached to it and she had run out of time to answer it. She was also a bit disconcerted by the fact that in the middle of the rotation from station to station there was a bell which indicated everyone should take a break of five minutes. Holly just sat awkwardly in front of the interviewer she was with at that time, and tried to make a little small talk, although in hindsight she thought her interviewer probably would have welcomed her shutting up!

HOLLY:

In fact, I believe it was emphasised prior to the start of the
circuit that we really did not need to talk to the interviewer
during the break. What can I say? I was a jumble of nerves and
adrenaline held together by the jelly baby I had eaten for
breakfast. Also, please don't bring up a violent Italian-
American crime family at any point in a medical interview,
before or afterwards. It rarely gives the right impression...

At **Sheffield,** Holly cringed at the memory of walking through a
curtained off MMI station area before they were ready and being told
sharply to wait outside, but nothing else went wrong in that nothing was
unexpected. Sheffield had an unusual station in that they got medical
students to play the '20 questions' game with the candidates. Holly
didn't guess a lobster or the Leaning Tower of Pisa in the two games
she played but it didn't seem to matter. She planned her other answers
meticulously so that she didn't waffle on and she timed her answers.
The interviewers did ask additional questions to get her to expand on
some of her answers when she was discussing volunteering experiences.
It was at Sheffield that parents and candidates were told that the current
MMI process at all universities means it is often the same candidates
who are offered places after interviews; so many will get 4 offers and
many may get no offers but this does not mean that they were not good
candidates. This is why universities like Sheffield operate a waiting list
whereby students are kept in reserve for spaces as they become
available.

HOLLY:

Sheffield were so lovely that they gave me the questions they were going to ask-although the additional questions did mean that you had to think on your feet. They were still related to the original question though so nothing too out of the blue. Follow up questions were also present in the Hull /York interviews- sometimes they like to make the interview more like a conversation. In this situation try to take a moment to think through the different arguments/ points of view you can mention. They will appreciate a thoughtful answer more than a waffled answer and so don't be afraid to take that pause to think your answer through (although you won't be penalised for a little bit of waffle!)

MMIs are noisy, so you need to practise interview questions and answers in places where there are distractions and background noise – like a shopping centre.

It is likely that your interviewer will _not_ have read your application. At each station there is a new stranger to impress who is meeting you for the first time, and so knows nothing about you. It is your job to reflect on your experiences and work them into your answer.

Interview Questions advice

HOLLY:

Like I've said before, the ISC Medical School book really does have some good advice and I would encourage you to look at their tips and tricks. However, I wanted to give my best shot at writing my advice about the questions I found particularly common or interesting at the interviews.

Firstly, make sure you are thoroughly familiar with the prospectus and the selling points of that particular university.

Pretty much every interview I went to expected you to explain why you wanted to go to their university in particular. This is when you can gush about the unique aspects of the course and the city and how well they suit you in particular. University is like a very suspicious Henry Hoover salesman. You need to convince him that you really want a Henry Hoover by showing him that you've listened to the ads and read the instruction manual. So, if the Cardiff university website says how proud they are of having a new and improved spiral curriculum you know you should probably say how that was a really attractive factor for you and why. Or if Sheffield says that they are one of the few universities in the UK that do dissection instead of pro-section you should say why that appeals to you so much. Have about 3-4 points about the course that you can expand on. It's quite a nice question as long as you've done your research.

So, here are some common questions you can get stuck into (but please don't think these are the only ones you'll be asked!)

Q. Lots of excellent applicants get no offers due to the high demand of the course. What will you do if you don't get a place to study medicine this year?

A nicer variation on the 'how do you cope with failure?' question. It's nicer because you don't have to think of an example where you've failed - they've given it to you. It was also a prime opportunity to explore my determination to do medicine.

I guessed that the answer they wanted wasn't 'roll up into a foetal position and rock back and forth' (although it's probably a perfectly understandable response in the short term). I reckoned they wanted me to show that I will bounce back from this setback, reflect on my mistakes, ask for feedback, fix and improve on what was wrong with my interview. Reflection is an incredibly important part of being a doctor as highlighted by the GMC's 'Reflective Practitioner - a guide for medical students'. Another great resource to read! (https://www.gmc-uk.org/education/standards-guidance-and-curricula/guidance/reflective-practice/the-reflective-practitioner---a-guide-for-medical-students)

I wanted to show that I was capable of starring in a 'Rocky' training montage, in which I'd beef up my application. I'd get better work experience, I'd do more volunteering, perhaps even start my own research project! I wanted to show that I would be determined enough to throw everything at it the second time round and if that didn't work I'd try to get in on a postgraduate Medical course (and hopefully that course would be at the same university I'm telling all this to (;). We want to show them that we are fully committed to this course and to them.

Q. Do you think that non-emergency services should be provided 7 days a week in the NHS?

This was an interesting/challenging question to be asked because it is in reference to a fairly complex 'hot topic' from 2015 rather than a more current one. (However, Sheffield gave me these questions prior to the interview so it wasn't really that mean.) Your current hot topics in the year you sit your MMIs will be highlighted to you by the Medic Portal.

During 2015 the Conservatives' manifesto said that they were committed to creating a 'truly 7 day NHS' where GPs would be open to patients for the full 7 days. This was incredibly controversial at the time as it was a politically driven reform and went against what those in the medical profession believed should be changed within the NHS. The controversy continued due to the Health Secretary's (Jeremy Hunt's) repeated claim that there were higher deaths in hospitals at the weekends, hoping to validate the policy. However, this claim was drawn from unreliable evidence and it was later discovered that 13 reliable, peer reviewed studies had been done to refute 'the weekend effect' when Hunt began making these claims. The BMA questioned if it would be properly funded and medical professionals argued that the money should be directed where it was really needed like improving access to key services, such as MRI and CT scans, as well as the need for improved staffing.

Putting in some context can be nice and is probably expected of you if you get a hot topic question like this prior to the MMI. I didn't go into it in as much detail as I've written above, I summarised it in a couple of sentences. But by giving context to your answer, you show that you have an interest in the world revolving around your future occupation.

However, I must admit that if I hadn't talked these questions through with my parents I would have been slower to clock that it was in reference to this controversy. This shows just how important it is to involve others in your MMI prep!

What I believe they really want from this question is for you to give an informed, balanced and evaluative answer. I weighed up the pros and cons of a 7 day NHS and then justified my opinion. I remembered that all reforms and choices we make as doctors should be made with the patient's best interest at heart and that was ultimately how I validated my opinion.

Q. Do you think it might ever be appropriate to breach a patient's confidentiality? Can you give any examples?

Another interesting question that required some research on my part and again brings up some controversial points. I encourage you to also research the exceptions for breaking patient confidentiality as highlighted in Good Medical Practice guidelines. Consent and patient confidentiality are important topics for a doctor and you may be queried on them.

This is one of the rare questions where I didn't think they would expect me to have an example to draw upon from my work experience as it is, fortunately, pretty rare for there to be sufficient reason to break patient confidentiality. My examples were more generalised: For example, if a patient were to describe that they were suffering from a mental health issue, like severe depression then they may be a risk to themselves or others. So, you may have to break patient confidentiality and inform the appropriate services.

You might use an event in a current news article as an example, at the time of my MMI there was a woman suing St. Georges Trust for not telling her that her father had died of Huntington's Disease, a strongly inheritable and fatal brain condition, which would have influenced her decision in deciding whether or not to abort her baby. The patient, the woman's father, specifically asked his doctors not to tell his daughter about his condition out of fear she would kill herself or have an abortion. This controversy raises tension between the competing interests of duty of care and the duty of confidentiality.

[For some background see **Huntington's disease: Woman who inherited gene sues NHS** *]*

https://www.bbc.co.uk/news/health-50425039

Q. While working at your Saturday job in a shop you find that one of your colleagues has arrived at work smelling of alcohol. They appear to be intoxicated, and you know that they drove to work. What actions would you take?

Wait, Marty have we gone back in time? Am I back in the UCAT? Because this sounds like a Situational Judgement question. If you've remembered anything about all the crazy antics medical professionals get up to in the SJ section of the UCAT you should be able to find questions like these pretty straightforward. (Side note: I'm intrigued to find out whether or not I'll catch my med student friend Karl steal IV equipment in real life.)

I will say this though, remember that both the customers in your shop (i.e. your patients) and your colleague (i.e. another health professional) needs protecting in this situation. Make sure that your colleague is safe and that his mental and physical health is supported appropriately. You gotta take care of your team, doc!

Q. Should Doctors use social media?

I had a variation of this question at more than one MMI... they really must not trust us with Instagram, huh?

However, with the rapid growth of social media and all the ethical dilemmas that can arise from it perhaps it's not so surprising that they want to make sure future medical students know that those crazy Christmas party pictures shouldn't make their way online. (I wish I could give a specific example but the craziest it gets at my Christmas parties is watching 'The Polar Express' twice over).

I think it's important to understand that mistakes made on social media can seriously affect patient-doctor relationships. It can also undermine the public's trust in the health service. There are numerous examples in the past about how there can be blurring professional boundaries due to inappropriate conduct on social media. Posting the wrong pictures or tweeting inappropriate comments could lead to loss of respect or cause conflict in a patient-doctor relationship. It can endanger that integral foundation of trust between doctors and patients.

An upside I recall mentioning was the fact that it can be an easy way to spread information to a wide audience on public health schemes, general health advice etc.

As you can see, I answered questions like these using a pros and cons method again in order to reach that all important fair and balanced conclusion. There are way more examples and points to make for this question. Once again you should check out the Good Medical Practice! It gives detailed guidance on responding appropriately as a doctor when using social media along with loads of other instructions on how to achieve (you guessed it) good medical practice. I cannot emphasise enough how it is a real beauty to read before your interview.

https://www.gmc-uk.org/ethical-guidance/ethical-guidance-for-doctors/doctors-use-of-social-media/doctors-use-of-social-media

https://www.gmc-uk.org/ethical-guidance/ethical-guidance-for-doctors/confidentiality---responding-to-criticism-in-the-media

At **Hull/York** the biggest difference was in the group interview. Candidates are randomly allocated the order in which they do the stations and one might expect them to perform better in the group task once they have been through a few stations together. You were kept in a specific group for the whole of the interview. Holly certainly felt there was a build-up of camaraderie as the day went on, but her group activity was the first task, so everyone was quite uptight. Afterwards, Holly was cringing at the fact that she kept saying, "Good point!" after the assertive students spoke and then suggested that some quieter people should have a chance to speak, but these probably were good traits to have displayed. There was an administrative task that seemed totally unrelated to medicine but required she pay close attention to some information. She did not realise until afterwards that there were some mistakes deliberately hidden in it.

HOLLY:

Yes, the group interview was… strange. I mean it was a great way to get insight into what a Problem Based Learning situation would be like but everyone was very intense and fighting to speak. In that situation my advice would be to stay calm, make sure you get to speak but offer a chance for someone else to speak too; say stuff like "no, it's okay, you go first". I think naturally people would have done this in a normal PBL session, and people did do this more as we went along, but as it was the first interview station it created quite a tense environment. I reckon people got scared that they wouldn't have a chance to contribute and so went in with their claws out. I found this pretty stressful but like with all my comments, this is only based on my own subjective experience and opinions of it.

In fact, when they asked for feedback at the end one girl said she really enjoyed the group interview because their group had done it last and so they had gotten to know each other by then. She said it was really relaxed and interesting. I hope your experience is like that!

By the time she got her interview in **Birmingham**, Holly had actually had an offer from Hull/ York. She was ecstatic! This certainly took the pressure off her final interview and this was the one in which she was most relaxed. There were no surprises in the interview and Holly had the advantage of having been through the three others although she was still nervous about her ability to perform well at all of the stations. It was the shortest interview taking up only an hour and a half. All of the others lasted about three hours.

Holly:

I really was incredibly ecstatic when I got that email from Hull York- and a sobbing wreck. Don't judge; so will you be, when you get your first offer. This was a very nice feeling to have and it meant I didn't blurt out something about the Mafia as I had in Cardiff, or stomp into the room before the bell invited me, as I had in Sheffield.

By the way, I heavily tortured myself and obsessed over my interviews for months and was highly certain I would end up with 4 rejections. Things aren't always as bad as they play out in your head. But really, try not to torture yourself over your performance in these interviews- in the words of Hannah Montana 'Que sera, sera'!

The Parental Role in the Interview Process

In the lead up to the interviews we practised what we thought might come up, and we encouraged Holly to speak to other medical students who had gone through the process on the phone. My brother, who had studied Medicine, spent an evening discussing the questions Sheffield had given her and generally we made sure she could show an awareness of current medical issues and could recite the NHS code of conduct. It was far better for Holly to be accompanied on her interviews by Simon than by me. Simon was once described by his boss as a man who laughs in the face of catastrophe, and by my father as a cock-eyed optimist. Better that, than Holly should suffer my company. I'd have been radiating anxiety with the intensity of the midday sun spilling heat on a prairie.

Instead, in Simon's company Holly was so laid back that on the morning of one interview she was still asleep when he knocked on her door expecting to take her for a leisurely breakfast. I'd have been volcanic in my reaction but Simon just gently woke her, suggesting she might make do with a bread roll rather than the full English he had been hankering after. Simon and Holly always stayed somewhere near the university the night before the interview and made sure they knew exactly where they needed to be and how long it would take to get there so that there was no chance of Holly being late – even if she overslept!

Parents or friends should spend time with their student, running through likely interview questions again and again. Make sure they can give clear and succinct answers to 'why medicine?' and 'why this university?'

Interviewees will be challenged by ethical dilemmas; previous work on the Situational Judgement Test will come in handy, along with knowledge of the BMA's Ethical Toolkit for Medical Students (see Appendix). Also make sure you are aware of, and up to date on any health stories in the news (find out what they are and have a considered opinion).

Time their answers (2 minutes each) and rehearse so they can speak fluently without hesitation, repetition or deviation!

HOLLY:

Tis' the night before the MMI and all through the house,

  your stomach is churning, you've ironed your blouse.

The suit is hung on the chimney with care,

  in hopes that an offer soon will be there.

The candidates are restless, sweating into their beds,

  while visions of parental disappointment dance in their heads.

I just ruined Christmas, didn't I? Sorry about that.

What I'm trying to get across is that the night before your MMI is going to be a little stressful especially if it's your first one, or if it's your only one. I remember that before my first MMI I couldn't immediately get to sleep and then I was stressed that I couldn't get to sleep which meant I was even more stressed and even more unlikely to get to sleep... A positive feedback loop of fear. Very festive. With regards to this particular problem my advice would be to try to slow your heart rate by taking deep, steady, even breaths. You could try square breathing (breath in for four seconds through your mouth and out for four seconds through your nose). If your mind really is racing perhaps try to read a book or do a repetitive action like knitting (yes, really!). Try to take your mind off tomorrow and get a goodnight's sleep. Which is way easier said than done.

Perhaps the best thing to remember when you're feeling stressed is that everyone is in the same boat. Everyone will be nervous and wishing for a couple of extra hours in bed when morning comes around on that MMI day. And ultimately, you will still be loved by your friends and family if you do mess this up! Which you won't!

My other tips for the night and day before your MMI:

1) *Often the MMIs take place in the morning and sometimes into early afternoon. You can usually book your time slots to your preference; I believe the earliest one for the Unis I applied for was 9:00.*
Remember to be fast when making that decision. Personally, I felt more comfortable with an earlier slot (I'm more awake and will have less time to chuck back expressos which make me shake like a dog on fireworks night) but the early slots are usually the first to go. If you are booked in for an early slot, it can be a real help if you're close by to the place that the MMI is being held so that you don't have to wake up super early. Usually this means driving down or getting the train the night before and booking into a hotel for the night. I appreciate that I was incredibly fortunate to have parents that were willing to spare this expense and it is not always feasible to do so. Don't worry if this is not an option for you- many people I was nervously chatting to when waiting to go into the MMI circuit told me that they had to get up early in order to travel for a couple hours to get there. On the bright side it will mean plenty of time to review your notes and get wide awake before your interview.

2) *Having a parent come down with me on the train and check me into the hotel and help me find where the MMI took place was incredibly helpful and reassuring. You want to do everything you can to minimise those anxiety factors and so having a sane, calm, helping hand to help me find my way around a big city was helpful.*

   (However, you might be a city slicker and not want your folks around which is completely understandable.)

3) *Plan where you're going to stay and what time you need to check out and if you'll walk to the university or if you'll get a cab or a bus. Add plenty of spare time in case buses or traffic foul up.*

   [How do you organise a space themed party? Planet! Heh, heh!]

4) *Look up the location of the MMI on Google maps and see how far it is to the train station or from the place you'll be staying.*

   Hopefully, you'll have done a couple months of preparation before this MMI. Bring your notes, flash cards and questions with you and go through them by yourself or get a friend or guardian to quiz you on them the night before, or on the train.

5) *Make sure your interview outfit is ironed, washed and smells of cinnamon. (Other smells are acceptable but who doesn't love cinnamon?) Hang it up as soon as you get into your hotel room.*

By the way, you'll want to look like one of those guys from the PPI compensation adverts. That means well brushed hair, natural make up, no flashy jewellery and a plain but serious suit. I can't remember seeing an MMI-er who wasn't in an impeccably well-ironed suit and sensible shoes which was as disappointing as it was unsurprising. (If you go to an MMI in sequined stilettos I can't promise you'll get an offer but you will gain my respect).

Finally - accept your anxiety!

A study done in 2016 by Gong L, Li W, Zhang D, Rost DH titled "Effects of emotion regulation strategies on anxiety during job interviews in Chinese college students" showed that accepting that you will be anxious on interview day will be more helpful than trying to ignore your anxiety. Instead of supressing that nervous tick, perhaps think of strategies like wiggling your toes instead of anxious fidgeting. This way you can hide some of that anxiety while still giving it an outlet.

Chapter 8

The Offers

Hull/York offered Holly AAB because she had an EPQ (at A or above), as long as she put them first. She would need AAA if she put them as her insurance choice. The B could be in any subject. The offer came in January.

Her other three offers were zapped out in February half term. First came an offer from Birmingham which was AAA.

This was swiftly followed by an offer of AAA from Cardiff.

In the same week Holly got an offer from Sheffield which was AAB (because she had the A-starred in EPQ) but unlike Hull /York this offer remained regardless of whether she put them as her firm or her insurance choice.

The Decision

Holly was in the enviable position of having to choose! It was really difficult to make the decision knowing that it was a crossroads in her life. Only she could decide. Initially, Holly put Sheffield first and

Cardiff second but the following day she came home and announced that she had decided to change it round and had called UCAS while at school. She had then resubmitted her application with Cardiff as her first choice and Sheffield as her insurance choice. Thinking she was going to go to Sheffield I had spent the weekend watching lots of YouTube videos about the city. I'd reinvigorated a love of Jarvis Cocker and had stomach flutters over plans to ride their paternoster lift, but I took the news in my stride.

I'd grown up in Hendy, a Welsh village just off the end of the M4. The trek up and down that motorway had been the bane of my life when my father had been alive. Still, trundling down the M4 to visit Holly would be a lot less arduous. I might look at the journey with a bit more enthusiasm over the next five years. Holly was now keen to learn Welsh and started on Duolingo as soon as she had changed her firm choice from Sheffield to Cardiff. By the end of the week she had learned how to ask "Dych chi'n gweithio fel tredanwyr?" "Do you work as an electrician?" and had experienced the joy of calling carrots 'moron'.

Simon and I had no qualms about the course at Cardiff versus the course at Sheffield and we were sure she would be happy at either university. At least, I thought, if she came a cropper in Cardiff, my good friend Delyth was near at hand and could give her directions if she got lost.

In reality, Holly was perfectly capable of organising her own life, she was no longer in need of my advice and had just proved that by making that final UCAS decision without consulting her parents.

Holly's tip to the Med Kids:

Please take your time when thinking about which universities to go to after you have gotten your offers! Don't rush!

Up until this point I had very much just wanted to do Medicine anywhere that would take me; I didn't care where or with whom. So, all my university decisions were pretty strategically based on who might interview me, up until this point. For the most part I think that this was the correct thing to do- your priority has to be securing those interviews. I think having an unfounded soft spot for a certain university is a trap a lot of people fall into when applying. Birmingham has a really impressive medical building that might tug on your heart strings like a 50s crooner but if its offer calculator says you are unlikely to be accepted for interview, please don't put it down.

However, once you've strategically identified the Med schools that are going to like you, go find out how much you like them. Make notes on what you did and didn't like and try to start thinking about what would be your top one pretty soon after you've perused them all.

Don't go at the end of the open days. I know that all you'll want to be doing at this point is revising but I think that it's important to fully feel what the University and the student unions can do in full swing. This isn't a one-sided relationship: you've put in or are going to put in so much effort trying to woo them so now let them woo you! If I had my time again, I'd like to have visited Sheffield and Birmingham when they weren't trying to pack up! So, don't squeeze 2 unis into one day; try to free up 4 days to see where you are potentially going to spend the next 5 years.

Personally, I flip-flopped like crazy between Sheffield and Cardiff. I never dreamed I would be so lucky to have to decide between them, so I never really considered comparing and contrasting them after visiting. Even after we tried to online, they were both so similar in standing that I was very unsure which to put first. So, between you and me, I actually decided that I'd let my grades decide which one I should go to- if I got AAA, it would be Cardiff and AAB would be Sheffield. (I came to the conclusion that I could not decide on my fate and very much had a Jesus Take The Wheel moment).

That said, I am confident that pretty much all Medical schools are going to be amazing so although you should take your time, don't worry too much about your decision in the end.

Chapter 9

Pandemic and Results

Aweek and a half after Holly sent off her decision, the
government announced that GCSE and A level examinations
were cancelled. My lovely hairdresser Kelly was round at the
time which was the most fortuitous thing that happened that day, given
we would be imminently in Lockdown. At least it would be a while
before I'd be forced to cut my own fringe. Holly had just read the
education secretary's announcement on her phone. She shoved it under
my nose as Kelly grappled with my bob. "Dude? Dude? Dude?" Holly
said, presumably to me, Kelly and Gavin Williamson. Like everyone,
Holly was shell shocked. We were about to be bombarded by the terms,
"unprecedented times", "the new normal", and evasive claims about
"the science." Everything had changed.

The coronavirus had been making its way through Europe, having
caused chaos in China and then Italy. Finally, at least a week later than
they should have, the government reacted to the fact that the UK was
rife with the pandemic. Both my daughters were affected by the
cancellation of exams; Holly's sister, Katie, was in Year 11. As the news
sunk in, Holly assumed that the cancellation meant she was straight into
university, as she had accepted her offer and there was no further
obstacle in the form of exams. She started spinning around the kitchen,

scaring the dog. Poor Katie was devastated. Both girls had been revising like the future of mankind depended upon it only to discover mankind's future was already screwed.

Of course, having an ingrained work ethic, plus a sense of disbelief, they carried on revising. Indeed, as schools went into lockdown and teaching went online no-one wanted to tell year 11 or 13 that it was ok to stop working. The government's shambolic reaction, knee jerking from a blasé response to a panicked cancellation of exams, had been decided upon without consultation with schools. Nobody in charge of the secondary schools knew any more than your average Joe knew from reading the news online or watching it on telly. Quite possibly, many year 11 and 13s in the country had never worked so hard as they did that Easter, before the government told everyone that any work done after March 19th shouldn't be included in any teacher assessment. At that point many parents probably switched from forcing their kids to produce their best work ever, to sending gifts and ingratiating notes to staff, combined with a menacing subtext. I joke, but it was far from funny. I wanted to thank Holly's teachers but I refrained from contacting any staff as I didn't want them to think I was trying to influence their decisions or trying to find out what they were going to give in their assessments. In fact, the only contact I had with any of Holly's teachers was when I wandered into her bedroom in my underwear looking for deodorant and realised I'd become part of a Zoom call with her Art class. At least I was wearing a clean bra.

As we found out more about the teachers' requirements, I thought the worst part of it was the need to rank order the children, something that would be very difficult when teachers couldn't even get together to look at examples of work. Presumably, they didn't have access to their own students' work as they weren't allowed into school unless they were on the rota, looking after key workers' children. I thought that it would be easier for rank orders to be fairer at A level than GCSE where numbers were fewer, but even then, teachers would be required to rank order children they hadn't taught, against children they had. Even within one school, fairness would be an impossible task, let alone trying to create parity between schools. The government said teachers would not be using mock exams, but, in reality, I couldn't imagine how else a rank order could be achieved. I have no idea how Holly and Katie's schools fulfilled the requirements but I sympathised with the difficulties that faced staff at this time.

Holly continued to have some online lessons with her teachers and classes during the lockdown period, where they encouraged the students to research topics and present them to each other. This was great because it meant that Holly was honing skills she would need in the first term of university. Holly now realised, as her peers did, that there was still a question mark over whether or not she would be allocated the grades needed for Cardiff, but we both thought it would take a very strange turn of events for her teachers to renege on her predictions at this crucial moment in time. At this point, like everyone else, we were oblivious to the mayhem that would be created by the so-called algorithm; so Holly had a fairly relaxed wait until August for her results to come through.

Lockdown

We were all safe at home together; at least there was no FOMO, apart from early on, when we had no toilet paper. Holly taught herself to play the guitar and binge-watched gangster films. I tried not to feel cheated that I had been building up for years to the way I would nurture my girls through these exams, the ultimate stressful period of their adolescence which had simply evaporated. Having been a secondary school teacher for 20 years, and then a GCSE tutor, I felt defined by GCSEs and A levels. My whole raison d'etre was blown out of the water. I had to re-assess.

Perhaps all that really mattered was that we painted pictures of rainbows and stuck teddies in our windows; that we shared bags of flour with our neighbours, and went jogging in the morning, so that we could spend all afternoon back in our pyjamas: watching Netflix, guzzling buckets of chocolate and cheap wine, lying comatose on the sofa. (That was just me – everyone else in the household was far more productive.)

The Friday before lockdown occurred, Simon came home from work with a dry cough. That weekend he had the shivers but by Monday he felt a lot better and we joked that he had had the virus just for the weekend. My dismissive attitude changed abruptly when five days later I developed my own cough, headaches and a sore throat like I'd been slashed across the jugular. I spent the next seven days in bed (too fatigued to do anything more than displace the pain with the horror of the Tiger King documentary, compelling as rubber necking a car crash.) I realised that I could no longer smell shampoo or soap the day before loss of smell was added to the list of symptoms. Luckily, Holly and Katie appeared to escape unscathed. I didn't get tested so I don't know for certain that Simon and I had the virus, but, even so, as I read about it every day with increasing concern, I felt more and more lucky that we hadn't experienced any breathlessness.

Like everyone else during lockdown, we couldn't forget the horror of people dying from this pandemic. This was the subtext to all of our community spirit and online kindness to each other. Holly was acutely aware of the role of newly qualified doctors in combatting the virus and of the importance of her vocation as never before. She continued to study human biology, taught herself Joni Mitchel songs on the guitar and painted the cells of the disease. It seemed as good a way as any to spend lockdown limbo.

Results Day

We spent an anxious night fretting over reports in the newspaper that suggested that 40% of results had been downgraded. I didn't know if Holly's school would be badly affected. We knew the last three years' results were good and knew (somewhat unfairly) that would be good for Holly, so we were cautiously optimistic. For once, Holly had no trouble getting up early and she logged on to her UCAS track at exactly 8.00a.m. She was in! The congratulations were there in black and white, English and Welsh. We yelped and squealed and a few tears of relief leaked out of my eyes. I searched the page anxiously for some kind of 'Confirm' button. Holly swished the cursor across the screen looking for one.

"Don't press decline!" I said, imagining the horror of a keyboard mistake at this point. There really was only a 'Decline' button, so she logged out, and we trundled off in the car to collect her results from school, soberly aware that some of my friends' kids had been more adversely affected by the government cock-up than Holly had. At school Holly found out that she had been awarded A* A* and an A in Chemistry (although this was upgraded to another A* once the U-turn came into effect and the grades the teachers had given students were fully restored.) She tumbled into the car with a flimsy bit of paper that sealed her fate.

It was official: Holly was a medical student at last!

Holly in her first year room with her first real stethoscope

Afterword & some Do's and Don'ts

I'm writing this three weeks into Holly's first term at Cardiff uni. She is living in Talybont South in a flat of four; two boys and two girls in a house comprising six flats. She has had most of her learning online. She says it is really interesting, though there is an immense amount of work to be done. Holly was really excited to see the back of us when we dropped her off. Inevitably, one of her flat mates has tested positive for Covid and she is currently forced to stay in the flat – for two weeks! Luckily, mobile phones and technology are helping her cope. With Cardiff being in local lockdown I don't know when I can see Holly in the flesh next, but it is important to let her live independently, at last.

Finally, I am going to sum up our experiences with a list of do's and don'ts.

Based on Holly's experiences, please:

- Research the different demands of each university, according to the admissions websites
- Store the information on a spreadsheet so that you can compare the differences and reflect on them
- Think ahead when choosing subjects to study, remembering that most universities are happy for the third subject to be non-science. In fact, some prefer this
- Research where there are appropriate volunteering opportunities in your area
- Plan ahead so that you can make use of the summer holidays after GCSE exams for medical related volunteering or shadowing
- Remember it takes a few weeks to apply for volunteering positions. A DBS form may need obtaining and referees may need contacting. Many places may want to interview in person

or on the phone. Training days may need attending before volunteering can begin

- Try to get experience in a variety of medical related settings
- See the value of a Saturday job in terms of communication skills, responsibility, and resilience
- Use on-line resources, go on courses if you can afford to (such as those offered by Medic Portal), and buy hard copies of books to supplement interview and aptitude test preparation.
- Give yourself plenty of time to revise for the aptitude tests and to prepare for the interviews
- Talk to everyone you meet about your need for volunteering or shadowing experiences and you'll be amazed how helpful friends of friends can be
- Buy (or clean) a suit for the interview, polish your shoes and get a haircut
- Rehearse possible interview questions with friends or parents so that you can answer the obvious questions fluently, in detail, but concisely
- Buy 'Student Nosh' cookbooks before going off to live in halls. All measurements are in mugs and with ordinary spoons. Includes a short list of equipment needed to make all the tasty recipes
- Learn to use a toilet brush before you leave home

Here are the don'ts. As you'll know from reading this book, I am guilty of all of them. Read them and enjoy feelings of superiority!

Based on my experiences, please:

- Don't freak out when you realise how complicated the process of applying for medicine is
- Don't complete forms or phone up institutions on behalf of your child
- Don't underestimate how much your child knows about the expectations and how to prepare
- Don't book your child on courses without discussing it with them first
- Don't feel resentful that you are spending your evenings as a taxi driver rather than putting your feet up with a glass of wine
- Don't repeatedly remind your child that other people have more volunteering experience or a greater chance of doing well in the aptitude test
- Don't gasp "Why did you say that?" spitting feathers while your child recounts the answers they gave to their interviewers
- Don't worry! What will be, will be! Ultimately, even if your child has to try more than once and take a circuitous route to studying medicine, tenacity will pay off!

Good luck and best wishes,
Elinor

Appendix:
Resources and Holly's views of them

Mastering the UCAT CRC Press The Medic Portal

A good initial guide to the examination that I got when doing the 1 Day Medic Portal UCAT course. Clearly lays out all answers and the logic behind them which is particularly good for Abstract Reasoning which will almost definitely be a new premise that you get examined on. Also, it's a good way for reminding you how to do some of the maths for the Quantitative Reasoning section if you haven't taken it for A Level.

Rating: 7/10

Score Higher on the UKCAT (fourth edition) by Kaplan

I really liked this one. It has a diagnostic test at the beginning which you should do pretty early on so that you can see how far you have to go to reach a respectable score. It also has a conversion table where you can see the approximate UCAT score you would get in each section according to how many questions you have answered correctly. Keep a track of every mock score or section scores so that you can see if you are improving. Great guide to talk you through the exemplar questions with tips. Some practice questions are also included.

I got this in addition to the online question banks Kaplan offered.

Rating: 7/10

Ultimate UKCAT Collection with over 2500 questions and solutions

Provides huge amount of practice which is great. It also includes 6 mock papers that you should try to do under time conditions- gets you to start thinking about how you are coping with the time management aspect which is a huge restraint when it comes to the UCAT.

The quantitative reasoning section has a few mistakes in it which can be frustrating but overall, it starts making you power through loads of questions.

Rating: 6/10

1250 UKCAT Practice Questions by ISC Medical

The holy grail that everyone who sits the UCAT will have and starts out with. These were really good for most of the sections in comparison to the other books I had although the quantitative reasoning section made me tearful when I used to time myself doing them. The QR section of this book is a lot harder than the actual exam so do not despair! But still try to do them all and the mock paper.

Rating: 8/10

Medify - the online question bank

- 10239 + Questions, with Decision Making section
- 8 Full Mocks and 18 Mini-Mocks
- With time tracking and predicted scores

Medify was the love of my life during the UCAT. I cannot emphasise enough how important it is to get some online experience of this exam because the timing, the calculator, the glaring blue screen is all the new and terrifying things that make the UCAT so damn tricky. It's really similar in layout to the real exam and it gives you a performance breakdown for every set of questions you do. It calculates your score for you so you don't even need to rely on Kaplan's conversion table. Truly, have you ever heard of something this beautiful?

I started using it about 5 weeks before I sat the exam but honestly, I think I would have been better off doing it 7 weeks before. That is my only regret for Medify- that I didn't use it sooner. Because even after ploughing through those questions for 5 weeks there were still a tonne I didn't get to attempt because it had such a large question bank.

Lots of people will say DO NOT USE THE ON SCREEN CALCULATOR in the UCAT which is understandable because it is so painfully slow. They are correct to recommend that you should try to do the majority of calculations on the whiteboard or in your head. However, practicing the keyboard shortcuts on Medify and using the number keypad to plug in those numbers were super helpful for doing some of the harder calculations in the QR section faster.

Rating: 10/10

Medical School Interviews by George Lee (2nd Edition), ISC Medical

Amazing, gorgeous, stunning. I truly did fall in love with this one during my interview preparation. The only downside is that so did everyone else. This is the guide to MMI interviews that every interviewee will likely have read cover to cover. It gives you background knowledge including a brief history of Medicine, key medical bodies, an overview of private and external healthcare companies as well as giving you a better understanding of how the NHS works in Britain. It also gives key issues, topics and scandals regarding Medicine prior to the time it was published (2013). By the time you do your interview ISC may have produced a new edition but because this was about 6 years out of date when I sat my first interview, it was important that I kept up to date with the newer issues in healthcare and didn't rely too heavily on the more dated ones in the book.

It takes you through all the different types of interview questions with key points you should mention, some of the answers also including exemplar responses from students, as well as the not-so-exemplar responses so you know your do's and don'ts. It has a separate section for how to handle the more practical stations at MMIs which have popped up in the past which is great at giving you a flavour of how wacky the MMIs can sometimes be. By doing the questions and reading the answers and logical explanations behind the answers you'll be able to get a real understanding of what the interviewers are looking for. This helps as on the day you can begin to try to understand the reasoning behind the question and give an appropriate response. Tips and acronyms to help you remember how best to approach and structure your answer are also included. Basically, you need this book for MMIs like Lorelai Gilmore needs coffee to function.

Rating: 10/10

Good Medical Practice (GMC)

https://www.gmc-uk.org/ethical-guidance/ethical-guidance-for-doctors/good-medical-practice

Useful (well, actually essential) knowledge for the SJT test and interviews – and for being a generally decent person and a good doctor.

Rating: 10/10

Key principles of ethics for medical students (BMA)

https://www.bma.org.uk/advice-and-support/ethics/medical-students/ethics-toolkit-for-medical-students/key-principles-of-ethics-for-medical-students

Even medical students need ethics – so learn them here!

Rating: 10/10

Acknowledgements

Holly and I would like to thank the GCSE teachers at St George's School, Harpenden, especially Rory Browne, Jane Crossland and Patricia Hess. We would also like to thank the sixth form staff at St Albans High School for Girls, especially Sarah Brown, Sally Legg, Helen Monighan, Joanna Scott, Sarah Stewart, Penny Wallis, and Caroline Weaver.

Much appreciated are those who helped Holly gain relevant shadowing or volunteering experience during Year 12. Thanks to Dominique Compton, Michelle Coleman, Richard Evans, Navina Evans, Nicky Mumford, Imelda Scowcroft-Tay and Jane Unwin.

Thanks also to the students who gave Holly insight into life at their universities: Izzie Beavis, Penny Ray, Molly Stewart and especially Elinor Laws.

And finally, thanks to our first readers: Fran Armstrong, Kate Jefford, James Kennedy, Usha Rowan, and especially Emma Beechey and Elizabeth Wittich.

And thanks to Simon and Katie Johns for putting up with us!

Printed in Great Britain
by Amazon